Smart Fish

Smart Fish

101 Healthful Recipes for Main Courses, Soups, and Salads

Jane Kinderlehrer

Newmarket Press
New York

THE NEWMARKET JANE KINDERLEHRER SMART FOOD SERIES

First Edition

93 94 95 96   10 9 8 7 6 5 4 3 2 1 PB
93 94 95 96   10 9 8 7 6 5 4 3 2 1 HC

Library of Congress Cataloging-in-Publication Data

Kinderlehrer, Jane
Smart fish: 101 healthful recipes for main courses,
soups, and salads/Jane Kinderlehrer—1st ed.
p. cm.— (The Newmarket Jane Kinderlehrer smart food series)
Includes index.
ISBN 1-55704-163-6 (pbk.) —ISBN 1-55704-164-4 (hc)
1. Cookery (fish)   2. Low-calorie diet—Recipes.
3. Salt-free diet—Recipes.   4. Low-fat—Recipes.
I. Title.   II. Series.
641.6'92—dc20   93-22796
CIP

Quantity Purchases
Companies, professional groups, clubs, and other organizations may qualify
for special terms when ordering quantities of this title. For information,
contact: Special Sales Department, Newmarket Press,
18 East 48th Street, New York, N.Y. 10017, or call (212) 832-3575.

Book design by Tania Garcia
Interior illustrations by Nina Duran

Manufactured in the United States of America

Contents

Chapter 5: The Fatter Fish

Introduction

OVERVIEW

WHY FISH IS A SMART FOOD CHOICE

Fish has long enjoyed a reputation as a brain food, probably because of its high content of phosphorus, a mineral the brain likes to play around with.

Even though they spend most of their lives in schools, there is no hard evidence that eating fish will enhance your chances of winning at "Jeopardy." But there is much evidence implying that you are smart to make fish a frequent part of your meal plan—if not for your brain, for your heart.

A VALENTINE FOR YOUR HEART…

Many studies have demonstrated that the special Omega-3 fatty acids in fish can:

- unclog arteries,
- lower levels of dangerous low-density cholesterol,
- lower levels of triglycerides, another group of blood fats that pose a threat to your heart,
- make the blood less prone to clotting,
- have a positive effect on cancer, diabetes, psoriasis, migraine headaches, arthritis, auto-immune diseases, and inflammatory diseases.

▼▼

...AND YOUR FIGURE

Fish has its merits for everyone. But, for those who wish to cut calories without sacrificing nutrients, fish is definitely a top-of-the-barrel catch. At approximately 100 calories in three ounces, fish is an attractive alternative to the 330 calories in an equivalent amount of meat.

Compared to fish oil, a typical vegetable oil provides as many as 60 percent more calories in attaining the same degree of total polyunsaturation in the diet. That's because, while vegetable oil may contain two, but never more than three sites of unsaturation, fish oils have four, five, or even six sites of unsaturation, thus giving fish oils a much greater degree of polyunsaturation than vegetable oils.

Fish do vary in caloric content, according to the amount of fat they contain. Four ounces of raw haddock, cod, and flounder provide only 85 calories. The same amount of swordfish or bluefish contain about 135 calories. But, even mackerel—which tops the list at 220 calories in four ounces—contains substantially fewer calories than an equal amount of meat.

Not only will fish, prepared with a smart flair, delight you with its succulent goodness, it will provide your body with almost all the important nutrients: protein, vitamins, minerals, and trace elements.

The vitamin content of fish, as with all fresh foods, is subject to seasonal change. Vitamin A content is highest in summer, but remains very high in the winter months, as compared with other foodstuffs.

Strange as it may seem, fish is low in sodium. This goes for ocean fish as well as freshwater fish, and is one reason why fish is so frequently prescribed for patients with high blood pressure. Fish also provides lots of phosphorus, necessary to the brain, as

I said earlier. Calcium, too, is found in fish in a form that is just as absorbable as that found in milk. In fact, the calcium-phosphorus proportion corresponds roughly to that of milk. But the very important and scarce mineral magnesium is higher in fish than it is in dairy products.

Fish also contributes to your iron stores. It is a common misconception that you must have red meat for good blood. Experiments have shown that, when seafoods are used as the main protein constituent of human diets, both red cell count and hemoglobin levels are maintained as well as with meat.

It is well known that fish are a marvelous source of iodine, so important to the thyroid gland. What is not so well known is that fish are an excellent source of copper, an essential mineral that is scarce in the usual fare, and that is necessary for making hemoglobin out of iron.

Fish certainly goes to the head of the class when it comes to "smart foods." But how you prepare that fish for the table can subtract from its nutritional score or can enhance it. Many fish recipes (not in this book) call for deep-fat frying or the addition of one or two tablespoons of butter. Not necessary.

In this book, we're playing it "smart." We have devised some highly pleasing recipes, rich in nutrients, and with added fiber—the one essential nutrient that fish leaves out of the swim. Try them. We think they will pleasure your palate, your waistline, and your well-being.

▼▼▼

SEAFOOD SAFETY–WHAT ARE THE FACTS?

An article in *Consumer Reports* magazine published early in 1992, raising questions about the quality, wholesomeness, and safety of the fish we are eating, has sparked a flurry of concern.

And rightly so. We should be concerned. After all, most of us are eating more fish to reap the benefits of a low-fat diet and the high content of the health-protective Omega-3 fatty acids. So what are the facts? Smart consumers want to know.

Just as in a political campaign, there is another side to the fish-safety story. Now, hear this: The American Institute for Cancer Research newsletter reports that:

- A recent study by the National Academy of Sciences gave our seafood a clean bill of health.
- According to the Centers for Disease Control, seafood accounted for only 5 percent of all food-poisoning cases reported between 1973 and 1987.
- The U.S. Food and Drug Administration (FDA) reports that seafood-related illnesses are decreasing even as Americans eat more seafood.
- The FDA recently conducted a special inspection of all seafood-processing plants in the United States. Inspectors checked to be sure that plants met sanitation and food-handling regulations, and they found violations in only a small percentage of cases.
- The FDA regularly analyzes seafood for pesticides and industrial chemicals. In 1992, it increased domestic sampling by 50 percent and doubled sampling of imports.

However, to eliminate even that small percentage of violations, many consumer organizations are backing legislation now before Congress designed to create a more comprehensive government system to regulate the seafood industry.

In the meantime, you don't have to limit your consumption of "smart fish." While bacteria can frequently be found on shellfish taken from waters tainted by raw sewage, fin fish normally are unaffected. All the recipes in this *Smart Fish* cookbook call for fin fish.

WHAT TO LOOK FOR WHEN YOU BUY FISH

If you, a family member, a friend, or a neighbor love to go fishing, you're in luck. Believe me, freshly caught fish, put on the grill the moment you dock your boat, is like a taste of heaven.

Lacking a home-grown fisherman, you might develop a friendly relationship with the person from whom you buy fish. Choose a reliable dealer on whom you can depend for top quality and honest judgment. Shop for clothes and accessories in a thrift shop if you're economizing, but never, never compromise on the quality of fish. Buy the best. The best is not necessarily the most expensive, but, most emphatically, insist on top quality.

Your nose and your eyes are your most important tools when you are looking for fresh, top-quality fish. If there is any odor at all, it should be mild and evoke the aroma of a fresh ocean breeze. Pass up any fish that smells *noticeably* fishy.

Top-quality fish looks as if it has just jumped out of the water. It should have a lustrous sheen and bright skin color. The eyes should be bright and full and never sunken. The gills should be reddish-pink, clean, and not sticky. The flesh of the fish should be firm, elastic, and moist. Scales should have a sheen and adhere tightly. When buying fillets, look for moist, glossy translucent flesh. Pass up fillets that are dry or slimy.

Buy fresh fish when it is in season in your locality. That's when it is best and is least expensive. Try less familiar varieties when they are abundant and inexpensive. The demand for favorite varieties frequently increases the price. As Georges Auguste Escoffier, the renowned French chef, pointed out years ago, "The culinary value of the fish has far less to do with the vogue it enjoys than the very often freakish whims of the public."

HOW MUCH SHOULD I BUY?

How much should you buy? As a general rule, figure six to eight ounces for each adult, a little less for children. Be sure to mentally calculate the weight of the fish after skin, bones, scales, etc., have been removed. Also, articulate clearly when ordering. I once asked for two pounds of bluefish fillet. What I got was a two-pound blue, filleted, which left me with only fourteen ounces of fish to feed four adults and one child.

Believe me, it's much better to have too much than too little. Leftover fish makes a great salad or tasty fish cakes.

MARKET FORMS

At the market, fish is available in these forms:

- Whole or round—fish as they come from the water
- Whole dressed—fish with scales, entrails, and usually the head, tail, and fins removed. Allow about three-quarters of a pound per person. Don't hesitate to ask for the head and carcass when you have a whole fish filleted. Use for stock. Be sure to eat the very tasty chunks of fish encased in the head. This was my Mom's favorite nosh. "It's what makes me so smart," she would say with a wink. When I order whole dressed fish, I specify that I want the head and the tail left on; this makes for a juicier, tastier dish. For squeamish eaters, remove the head before serving.
- Pan dressed—the term referring to smaller fish weighing about one pound, with head, tail, and fins removed— except for very small fish like smelt, which are usually sold whole. Allow a half pound per serving.
- Steaks—cross-section slices, about $5/_8$ to 1 inch thick, of large, firm-fleshed fish such as salmon, swordfish, halibut, and cod. One pound will serve two or three.

- Fillets—boneless sides of fish cut lengthwise away from the backbone and rib cage. One pound should serve three.
- Frozen fish—fish that is frozen stiff and has no signs of having been refrozen or of freezer burn. (Light-colored spots indicate freezer burn. This occurs when the fish is not packaged tightly.) You know that fish has been thawed and refrozen when it is contorted in shape. Once a frozen fish is thawed, it must be cooked quickly. I like to remove frozen fish from the freezer about a half hour before cooking so that it will still be somewhat solid when it hits the heat. Granted that frozen fish is not so tasty as fresh fish, but it's better than no fish.

STORING

Because fish is so perishable, it is always displayed on ice but, if you're not going to cook it immediately, store it in your refrigerator on a bed of ice—for no more than 24 hours. This reduces the temperature, bringing it close to zero, but it doesn't freeze it.

If you plan to freeze your own catch, be sure to set the freezer at zero degrees. If freezer space is at a premium, remove head and bones and make stock. Fillet the fish and freeze it along with the stock.

▼▼▼

DISCOVER THE MANY WAYS TO PREPARE SUCCULENT FISH

If every time you think fish, you reach for the frying pan, you'll be amazed and delighted with the moist, flavorful fish you will bring to the table when you try other techniques such as:

STEAMING. In a covered pot, a wok, or a fish poacher, place the fish on a rack above a swirling liquid that may be water, wine, or flavored broth. This is an excellent method for preserving the delicate flavor of lean fish, either fillets or small whole fish. Figure one minute for each ounce of fish, but test early to prevent overcooking.

POACHING. This method differs from steaming in that the fish is completely immersed in an aromatic broth and simmered, not boiled, for about 6 to 8 minutes per pound. The fish should be wrapped in a double layer of moistened cheesecloth, allowing extra length at each end for easy removal.

BROILING. This is an excellent way to develop flavor in fatty fish, small fish left whole after dressing, fish cut into chunks, whole fish that are butterflied, and fillets and steaks. Fish to be broiled should range in thickness from $1/_2$ inch to $1^1/_2$ inches. Thicker than $1^1/_2$ inches would dry out before being fully cooked. (For thicker fish, baking is a more effective method.) To broil, place the fish on a perforated rack that fits over a pan. The rack should be oiled, buttered, or sprayed with non-stick cooking spray. Broil about 4 inches below the source of heat. Thick steaks and whole fish should be turned over with a wide spatula.

BAKING. Any and every kind of fish can be baked. This is the most expedient way to cook large, whole stuffed fish; but smaller fillets and steaks may also be baked. Place the fish in a

▼▼

baking dish that has been oiled, buttered, or sprayed with non-fat cooking spray, and bake, uncovered, in an oven preheated to 350–375 degrees. Test frequently to determine doneness.

FRYING. Pan-frying, oven-frying, and deep-frying are quick cooking methods that contribute a nice crunchy exterior, a moist interior, and lots of flavor. Choose small whole fish or fillets for frying. (The coating on thick pieces of fish tends to burn before the fish is cooked through.) To pan-fry fish, bread it lightly, then place it in a skillet with a thin layer of heated oil over medium heat and fry it briefly on both sides until golden brown.

Oven-fried fish is also lightly breaded, placed in a baking dish that has been oiled, buttered, or sprayed with a non-stick cooking spray and then placed in a hot oven (450 to 500 degrees). The fish cooks quickly and does not have to be turned.

Deep-fried fish, reminiscent of the Fish 'n Chips that was consumed in huge quantities in my New England hometown, is dipped in batter, then cooked in very hot oil (370 degrees) in a deep-frying pan until golden brown.

LEFTOVER FISH

I always prepare more fish than we can eat, in order to ensure there will be leftovers. We love it in cold salad with a tart dressing, or made into a seafood quiche. Sometimes I mix the fish with bread crumbs, wheat germ, some mashed potatoes, and seasonings, or bind the mixture with a beaten egg and fill the house with the appetizing aroma of sizzling fish cakes!

MICROWAVING FISH

Remember the Canadian rule of ten minutes cooking time for every inch of thickness of the fish? Forget it when you're microwaving. Fish in the microwave cooks in about half the time it takes in a conventional oven—about 4 minutes a pound on high or one minute for every 3¹/₂ ounces.

The recipes in this book that call for baking or poaching will do very well in the microwave and will be lower in calories because it is not necessary to add fat or to grease the casserole.

Because there is so little evaporation of liquids in the microwave, reduce the amount of liquid called for in the recipe by about one-third. Cover the fish with a damp paper towel, waxed paper, or microwave-safe plastic wrap. For added flavor, wrap the fish in romaine lettuce or, if you relish a slightly tart flavor, as I do, wrap the fish in fresh sorrel leaves.

When arranging the fish in the microwave-safe casserole, be sure to place the thinnest part in and the thickest part out, or overlap the thinner ends so that the fish is of uniform thickness.

If you're microwaving a whole fish, it's a good idea to cover the head and tail with aluminum foil to protect them from scorching and prevent the eyes from popping.

Microwave cooking calls for split-second timing. When the flesh begins to lose its translucence, remove it from the micro-oven and let it stand, covered, for a few minutes. It will then complete its cooking and be tender, flaky, and rich in good satisfying flavors.

CHAPTER 1
APPETIZERS

▼▼▼

Appetizers can be a prelude to the main meal, or, served in larger portions, can be the meal itself. Any savory dish can be served as an appetizer. Just serve it in small quantities or as a finger food, so that it piques the appetite but does not satisfy it. I especially like to serve fish appetizers when the main meal does not include fish. In this way I can assure that my family will be getting the important nutrients that only fish can provide.

In the following ten recipes I have put the emphasis on herring and sardines because these fish are under-utilized as main dishes, yet they provide many valuable nutrients. Sardines, for instance, which are really undersized herring, pack a whale of a lot of good nutrients into their tiny little bodies. Their protein content is high; they provide all the B vitamins except thiamine, with unusually high levels of folate and vitamin B_{12}. Sardines are one of the few food sources of vitamin D, the nutrient essential to the utilization of calcium. And because you consume the bones in these delicate little fish, you also get a good supply of calcium.

For those who wish to cut calories without sacrificing nutrients, sardines provide a tasty alternative to other sources of protein. Even when packed in oil, they contribute a modest 186 calories for an average serving. To further limit the calorie content, pour off the oil. Calories will drop to 122. To cut down on the sodium, rinse in cold water.

The recipes that follow will help you devise a tray of appetizers that tease the appetite. Bear in mind that with appetizers the presentation can also stimulate the appetite. Arrange them attractively on pretty trays. Consider texture and color to please the eye as well as the palate. Go creative with colorful garnishes: bright orange carrot curls, sprigs of green parsley or dill, ruby-red radish roses, green and red pepper rings, black and green olives, and sprigs of whatever fresh herbs are growing on your windowsill or in your garden—basil, thyme, oregano, mint, or chervil.

Mushrooms Stuffed with Tuna and Water Chestnuts

An enticing tidbit, these are easy to prepare and low in calories.

1 pound fresh mushrooms (large ones preferable)

1 can tuna (6 $1/2$ or 7 ounces) in oil, drained

2 teaspoons reduced-sodium soy sauce

$1/4$ cup chopped water chestnuts (almonds may be substituted)

$1/2$ teaspoon powdered ginger

Wipe the mushroom caps with a damp paper towel. Remove stems and reserve for another use. Place the mushroom caps, top side down, on a baking sheet that has been lightly greased or sprayed with a non-stick baking spray. In a small bowl, combine the remaining ingredients. Spoon this mixture into the mushroom caps. Bake, uncovered, at 350 degrees for 5 to 6 minutes, until steaming hot. Serve at once.

To microwave: Place the mushrooms on a round micro-safe platter covered with a double layer of paper toweling; cover loosely with wax paper. Microwave on high for 2 minutes or until hot.

Yield: 12 appetizer servings.

*Each stuffed mushroom provides: 49 cal, 5 g pro,
1.2 g unsat fat, 20 mg sodium, 10 mg chol.*

Tuna with Marinated Artichoke Hearts

The artichokes provide the marinade that brings an explosion of flavors to this piquant dish.

1 jar (6 ounces) marinated artichoke hearts

$1/2$ cup whole pitted olives

$1^{1}/_{2}$ cups sliced mushrooms

$1/3$ cup olive oil

2 tablespoons red wine or balsamic vinegar

2 tablespoons lemon juice

1 large clove of garlic, minced

$1/8$ teaspoon freshly ground pepper

$1/2$ teaspoon dill weed

1 can ($6^{1}/_{2}$ ounces) chunk light tuna,
water-packed and drained

$1/2$ teaspoon dill weed

crisp romaine leaves

$1/2$ cup sliced almonds, lightly toasted

Drain and reserve the artichoke marinade. Arrange artichokes, olives, and mushrooms in a 3-quart shallow baking dish. In a screw-top jar, combine the reserved marinade, oil, vinegar, lemon juice, garlic, pepper, and dill. Cover the jar and shake it well. Pour it over the vegetables. Cover the dish and refrigerate for at least one hour.

Drain the marinade into a cruet or small pitcher. Fold the tuna into the marinated vegetables. Spoon onto small plates lined with romaine. Pour additional marinade dressing over each serving. Garnish with toasted almonds.

Yield: 10 servings.

Each serving provides: 115 cal, 5.2 g pro,
2.2 g sat fat, 4 g unsat fat, 8.4 mg chol.

Herring Salad with Potatoes, Beets, and Apples

Just recalling this dish makes my mouth water. It's that sensational and so easy to put together.

1 cup pickled herring
2 beets, boiled, or 1 can of sliced beets
4 medium-size potatoes, boiled and cooled
1 large Granny Smith apple, cored but not peeled
3 slices medium-size red onion
$^1/_4$ cup vinaigrette dressing
2 tablespoons chopped walnuts

Discard the onion slices that come with the herring and drain. Cut the herring, beets, potatoes, and apple into half-inch cubes. Dice the onion. Combine all ingredients in a bowl. Add vinaigrette to taste and sprinkle with walnuts.

Yield: 10 servings.

Each serving provides: 114 cal, 5.1 g pro, .4 g sat fat, .4 g unsat fat.

Sardine and Cottage Cheese Spread

Sardines are little, but oh boy, they pack a nutritional wallop that's hard to beat. For a lovely marriage of distinctive flavors, enjoy this spread on toast points or toasted pita, or stuff it into celery.

2 cans (3¹/₄ ounces each) sardines
¹/₂ cup low-fat ricotta or drained cottage cheese
2 shallots, scallions, or ¹/₂ small onion; finely minced
1 tablespoon chopped parsley
¹/₂ teaspoon paprika
pinch of cayenne pepper
2 tablespoons lemon juice

Drain sardines well. In a flat bowl, mash the sardines. Combine with the remaining ingredients and mix to blend. Makes ³/₄ cup.

Yield: 8 servings.

Each serving provides: 36.3 cal, 4 g pro, .8 g fat.

Darling Little Cheese Balls

1 can (3¹/₄ ounces) sardines
4 ounces reduced-calorie cream cheese
1 teaspoon Worcestershire sauce
2 gratings of pepper or to taste
¹/₂ cup finely chopped nuts (any kind)

Drain sardines well. In a bowl, mash them with a fork. Add the cheese, Worcestershire sauce, and pepper. Mix until well blended and smooth. Cover bowl and refrigerate until chilled. Form into small balls of about ³/₄-inch-diameter. Roll in chopped nuts. Place cocktail pick in each ball. Chill and serve.

Yield: 15 balls.

Each cheese ball provides: 40 cal, .66 g pro, 1 g sat fat, 1 g unsat fat.

Curried Tuna Pinwheels

This easy-to-prepare hors d'oeuvre is a taste sensation. It can be prepared ahead, up to the broiling. Broil just before serving.

1 can chunk-style tuna, packed
in water and drained

$1/_2$ teaspoon curry powder

1 tablespoon grated onion

6 tablespoons plain yogurt

2 tablespoons reduced-calorie mayonnaise

14 slices fresh whole-grain
or enriched white bread

paprika

In a medium-size bowl or food processor, blend together the tuna, curry powder, grated onion, yogurt, and mayonnaise until creamy. Trim crusts from the bread. (Reserve them and toast them lightly for bread sticks.) Spread each slice of bread with the tuna mixture. Sprinkle with paprika.

(cont.)

Roll up each slice jelly-roll fashion. Wrap securely in waxed paper and chill for 6 hours or overnight. Before serving, slice each roll crosswise into 3 pieces.

Place on cookie sheet lined with parchment paper or sprayed with cooking spray. Broil until golden, about 3 minutes; turn and toast the other side. Serve hot.

Yield: 42 pinwheels.

Each pinwheel provides: 24.7 cal, 2 g pro, .5 g fat.

Chopped Herring with Applesauce

This is an easy way to make the lovely chopped herring so popular in Jewish cuisine.

1 cup pickled herring

$^1/_4$ cup chopped red onion

$^1/_2$ cup unsweetened applesauce

Drain the herring and remove onions. In food processor, blend together the herring, red onion, and applesauce. Add additional applesauce if needed, to make a light, chunky texture.

Yield: 2 cups.

*Each tablespoon provides: 39.7 cal, 2.4 g pro,
.28 g sat fat, .28 g unsat fat.*

Pickled Salmon

2 $\frac{1}{2}$ cups water

1 cup white vinegar

4 onions, sliced

2 teaspoons herbal seasoning

2 tablespoons honey

1 tablespoon pickling spices

2 pounds fresh salmon steaks, cut in 1-inch chunks

In a medium-size saucepan, combine water, vinegar, and half of the sliced onions. Bring to a boil and continue on a slow boil for 15 minutes. Add the herbal seasoning, honey, pickling spices, and salmon chunks. Simmer for 10 minutes or until salmon flakes easily with a fork. With a slotted spoon, remove the fish to a deep bowl.

Layer the remaining onion slices between the chunks of salmon. Pour the cooking liquid, unstrained, over the fish and cover tightly.

Yield: 8 to 10 servings.

*Each of 10 servings provides: 150 cal, 22 g pro,
3.8 g unsat fat, 52 mg sodium, 74 mg chol.*

Salmon Torta Appetizer

This dish works just as well with tuna. It is excellent served either hot or at room temperature—wonderfully welcome at bring-a-dish parties.

1 can (7 ½ ounces) pink salmon

4 eggs

1½ cups unpeeled shredded zucchini

¼ cup oat bran

¼ cup wheat germ

¼ cup whole-wheat pastry flour

2 tablespoons lecithin granules (optional)

½ cup plain yogurt

½ cup diced onion

1 teaspoon tarragon

2 tablespoons sesame seeds

(cont.)

Drain the salmon and reserve.

In the bowl of food processor, combine the eggs, zucchini, oat bran, wheat germ, flour, lecithin granules, yogurt, onion, and tarragon. Process to combine ingredients. Add the salmon and mix well. Pour the mixture into a $1^1/_2$-quart shallow glass baking dish. Drizzle sesame seeds on top. Bake in a 350-degree oven for 35 minutes or until firm and golden. Cut into one-inch-square pieces.

Yield: 35 pieces.

Each piece provides: 22 cal, 2.6 g pro, .3 g sat fat,
.5 g unsat fat, 30 mg sodium, 34 mg chol.

Shad Roe Appetizer

This zippy appetizer tastes sinfully good but, in fact, is very low in calories and fat.

1 shad roe

1 cup dry white wine

1 teaspoon herbal seasoning

$1/4$ teaspoon freshly ground pepper

2 tablespoons mustard

1 tablespoon horseradish

In a saucepan combine the roe, wine, and seasonings. Heat to the boiling point, then simmer for about 20 minutes or until the roe is cooked through. Drain and chill for several hours in the refrigerator. In a small glass bowl, combine the mustard and horseradish.

Slice the roe thin and serve on crackers spread with the horseradish sauce.

Yield: about 10 slices.

Each slice provides: about 10 cal, 1.5 g pro, .3 unsat fat, 3.6 mg sodium.

CHAPTER 2
SALADS

Fish salads can be made in infinite variety, and they give you a wonderful opportunity to combine complementary nutrients, textures, and flavors. Salads bring fiber, color, and crunch to the protein and the Omega-3 fatty acids that you get in fish.

Any cooked fish can be a wholesome ingredient in a salad. In the following recipes I have put the emphasis on tuna and salmon because they turned out to be the best fish for lowering LDL, or "bad" cholesterol, and because these fish are generally available in cans.

Several different kinds of fish are sold as tuna. The lightest of these, albacore, is labeled "white meat." All the others are labeled "light meat."

The three different forms in which tuna is packed refer to the size of the pieces in the can: chunk-style, flaked, and grated. All represent good-quality tuna. Always check the label when you buy tuna to see if it's packed in water or oil. Water-packed tuna has less oil and fewer calories than the oil-packed, even when the oil-packed is well drained.

To reduce the salt content of canned tuna, dump it into a strainer and give it a cold-water shower.

Tuna and Pasta Salad
with Pine Nuts and Red Peppers

If pine nuts are unavailable, use sunflower seeds or chopped almonds.

1 tablespoon olive or canola oil

$1/2$ cup pine nuts

2 cloves garlic, minced

1 large tomato, peeled and coarsely chopped

One $6^{1}/_{2}$- to 7-ounce can water-packed tuna, drained

One 5-ounce jar roasted red
peppers or pimentos, cut in strips

$1/2$ cup pitted black olives, coarsely chopped

2 tablespoons balsamic or red-wine vinegar

freshly ground pepper, to taste

1 pound regular or spinach fettuccine or linguine

2 tablespoons minced parsley

(cont.)

In a heavy skillet, heat the oil. Add the pine nuts and cook until lightly browned, about 2 minutes. Stir in the garlic and cook until golden, about 1 minute more. Stir in the tomato. Transfer the mixture to a large bowl. Stir in the tuna, red peppers, olives, vinegar, and pepper. At this point, the tuna sauce can be covered and allowed to stand at room temperature for up to 2 hours.

Meanwhile, cook the pasta according to package directions until it is *al dente.* Drain in colander, then add the pasta to the tuna sauce and mix well. Sprinkle with the parsley. Serve at room temperature.

Yield: 6 servings.

Each salad provides: 216 cal, 11.4 g pro, .2 g sat fat, 2 g unsat fat.

Salmon Salad with Yogurt and Cucumber

In this recipe, yogurt provides all the moisture needed and a touch of cool tartness that accents and enhances the flavor of the salmon. Serve on crisp salad greens or in pockets of lightly toasted whole-wheat pita.

1 cup cooked or canned salmon, flaked

1 small cucumber, diced

6 tablespoons plain yogurt

2 teaspoons lemon juice

1 tablespoon chopped scallions or chives

salad greens

whole-wheat pita, halved

In a glass bowl, combine all the ingredients except the salad greens and pita. Chill.

Yield: 3 servings.

Each serving provides: 166 cal, 12.4 g pro, 2 g sat fat, 4 g unsat fat.

Tuna and Potato Salad Niçoise

This Mediterranean salad with its built-in salad dressing is a most satisfying one-dish meal. Enjoy it with a hunk of crusty Italian bread or a toasted whole-wheat pita.

2 tablespoons dry white wine

2 tablespoons wine or balsamic vinegar

$1/2$ teaspoon pepper, or to taste

$1/3$ cup olive oil

2 tablespoons minced green onions or chives

1 tablespoon minced parsley

$1/2$ teaspoon crushed oregano

8 medium-size potatoes, cooked, then peeled and sliced

Boston lettuce or romaine leaves,
or a combination of salad greens

1 cup green beans, cooked crisp but tender

1 can ($6^{1}/2$ ounces) water-packed tuna, drained

3 hard-cooked eggs, quartered

In a large bowl, combine wine, vinegar, and pepper. Stir in the oil. Remove and reserve $1/4$ cup of this dressing.

To the remaining dressing in the bowl, stir in the onions and parsley. Add the potatoes and toss gently until each slice is coated with dressing. Cover and refrigerate 2 hours to allow flavors to meld. To serve, line a platter with lettuce leaves; arrange potato salad, beans, tuna, and eggs on the lettuce. Pour reserved dressing over all.

Yield: 4 servings.

Each serving provides: 416 cal, 30 g pro, 3 g sat fat, 22 g unsat fat.

Tuna Ambrosia Salad
with Pineapple and Raisins

A delightful explosion of flavors, this salad is wonderful for a bridge or mah-jongg luncheon or a romantic patio repast. It provides a whole alphabet of wholesome nutrients to put energy in your body and a twinkle in your eye.

$^1/_2$ cup low-fat plain yogurt

2 tablespoons unsweetened flaked coconut

$^1/_4$ cup raisins

1 teaspoon curry powder

1 can water-packed chunk light tuna, drained

1 can (8 ounces) crushed pineapple, drained

1 cup alfalfa sprouts

1 can mandarin oranges, drained

$^1/_4$ cup toasted pine nuts, chopped
almonds, or sunflower seeds

In a bowl, mix together the yogurt, coconut, raisins, and curry powder. Fold in the tuna and pineapple. Line four salad plates with alfalfa sprouts. Arrange orange sections around the outer edge of the sprouts. Spoon the tuna mixture into the center. Sprinkle each salad with pine nuts, almonds, or sunflower seeds.

Yield: 4 servings.

Each serving provides: 190 cal, 17.2 g pro, 1.6 g sat fat, 2.1 g unsat fat.

Polynesian Tuna Salad

2 tablespoons mayonnaise

2 tablespoons yogurt

1 tablespoon lemon juice

1 can (6½ ounces) tuna fish, drained

2 tablespoons raisins or currants

2 tablespoons chopped celery

4 slices canned pineapple, drained

½ cup chopped, toasted almonds

sweet red pepper to garnish

In a mixing bowl, combine mayonnaise, yogurt, and lemon juice. Add tuna, raisins, or currants, and then celery. Mix to combine ingredients and refrigerate. To serve, place pineapple slices on top of chopped almonds; top with tuna mixture and sweet red pepper.

Yield: 2 to 4 servings.

Each serving provides: 215 cal, 18 g pro,
4.3 g sat fat, 11 g unsat fat, 82 mg sodium, 42 mg chol.

Hot and Cold Grilled Salmon Salad

I enjoyed this salad at Parks' Seafood Restaurant in my hometown, Allentown, Pennsylvania. Fred Parks, the chef, graciously shared the recipe with me and I am happy to share it with you.

4 salmon fillets (4 to 5 ounces each)

$^1/_2$ teriyaki sauce

4 cups salad greens (using a mixture of romaine, parsley, and spinach)

4 pineapple slices (fresh or canned)

2 red onions, thinly sliced

3 tablespoons pineapple juice

4 scallions, coarsely chopped

Place the salmon in a shallow bowl and brush each piece with the teriyaki sauce. Cover the dish and allow the fish to marinate for at least one hour. Prepare the salad greens and refrigerate.

Cut each pineapple slice into four chunks. Alternate the

pineapple chunks and the onion slices in a circle around the greens.

Grill the salmon and broil it about 6 minutes on one side. Brush it with the reserved marinade; turn and broil 4 minutes on the flip side.

To prepare the dressing, bring the reserved marinade to a boil, then simmer for a few minutes. Combine 3 tablespoons of the marinade with the pineapple juice and whisk together.

Place the hot salmon on the chilled greens. Sprinkle with the scallions and drizzle with the dressing.

Yield: 4 servings.

Each serving provides: 295 cal, 5.34 g pro,
5 g sat fat, 5.4 g unsat fat, 85 mg sodium, 66 mg chol.

CHAPTER 3

GUMBOS,
CHOWDERS,
AND OTHER CHOICE MEDLEYS

In this chapter you will discover the many tantalizing ways in which fish can bring you new culinary pleasures and nutritional advantages.

While fish is a complete protein food, providing all the essential amino acids plus a whole roster of vitamins and minerals, it does lack fiber. When you combine fish with vegetables and grains—in the form of gumbos, stews, or chowders—you must provide the missing element. Doing so, you will also make a little go a long long way. And when prices are sky-high, that is no small consideration.

Fish Gumbo with Bananas

You may never have thought of combining fish and bananas, but you will find that the bananas add a pleasant, sweet counterpoint to the tartness of the tomatoes.

2 tablespoons butter or oil

$1/2$ cup chopped onion

$1/4$ cup finely chopped green pepper

1 clove garlic, minced

1 tablespoon flour

2 cups chicken or vegetable broth

2 cups chopped tomatoes

$1/3$ cup chopped parsley

1 small bay leaf

$1/4$ teaspoon thyme

$1/8$ teaspoon freshly ground pepper

2 pounds fish fillets, cut into 2-inch chunks

1 teaspoon lemon juice

1 teaspoon reduced-sodium soy sauce

$1/8$ teaspoon cayenne pepper

4 bananas, cut into 1-inch chunks

(cont.)

In a large, heavy pot, heat the butter or oil. Add onion, green pepper, and garlic. Cook about 5 minutes or until soft. Add flour and cook for 2 minutes, stirring constantly. While stirring, pour in the broth. Add the tomatoes, parsley, bay leaf, thyme, and pepper. Bring to a boil, reduce the heat, and simmer, partially covered, for 20 minutes. Add fish and simmer for another 10 minutes. Discard the bay leaf. Stir in lemon juice, soy sauce, cayenne, and bananas. Serve with hot cooked brown rice.

To microwave: If you're a calorie counter, eliminate the fat. Fish will remain moist. In a 4-quart micro-safe casserole, micro-cook the onion, pepper, and garlic with one tablespoon broth or water for about 2 minutes on high and uncovered. Stir in the flour. Add only 1¹/₂ cups broth, the tomatoes, parsley, bay leaf, thyme, and pepper. Micro-cook for 8 minutes. Add the fish. Microwave, covered with vented plastic wrap, on high for 4 minutes. Proceed as in conventional recipe above.

If you prepare this dish without the fat, the calorie count drops to 360, the fat drops to zero, and the sodium to 383 mg.

Yield: 6 servings.

Each serving provides: 400 cal, 32 g pro, 1 g sat fat, .5 g unsat fat, 483 mg sodium, 60 mg chol.

Salmon Spaghetti

This sounds far out, doesn't it? Well, don't knock it. It is tasty, immensely satisfying, and so easy to prepare—even on the spur of the moment.

1½ cups sliced mushrooms

¼ cup sliced green onions

2 tablespoons butter or olive oil

1 can (15½ ounces) pink salmon with liquid

3 tablespoons dry white wine

1 pound whole-wheat or spinach spaghetti, cooked

1 cup plain yogurt

1 tablespoon whole-wheat flour

⅛ teaspoon freshly ground pepper

Sauté mushrooms and onions in butter or oil over low heat until vegetables are just tender. Add salmon, with its liquid, and the wine. Simmer for 3 minutes. Combine yogurt, flour, and seasonings. Stir into the salmon mixture in the skillet. Cook, stirring, for 3 minutes longer. Serve over the hot cooked spaghetti.

Yield: 4 servings.

Each serving provides: 401 cal, 33 g pro, 1.6 g sat fat,
.9 g unsat fat, 521 mg sodium, 62 mg chol.

Hearty Fish Stew

When you have a whole fish filleted at the market, be sure to ask for the head and carcass. They're great for fish stock, soups, and stews, as used in the following recipe.

bones, head, and skin of any fish, preferably salmon

6 cups water

1 onion, chopped

2 tablespoons butter

2 ribs celery, diced

2 potatoes

1$^1/_2$ cups flaked cooked fish

minced parsley for garnish

Place fish bones, head, and skin in a soup kettle with the water. Allow to simmer for 30 minutes. Strain and discard fish scraps. Sauté onion in butter until limp. Add celery and cook briefly. Dice potatoes, add to broth, and simmer until tender.

Add flaked fish. Simmer a few more minutes to heat the fish. Serve hot, garnished with parsley.

Yield: 6 to 8 servings.

Each of 6 servings provides: 133 cal, 6.5 g pro,
1.6 g sat fat, .9 g unsat fat, 66 mg sodium, 20 mg chol.

Elegant Tuna Bisque
with Flaky Puff-Pastry Top Hat

This easy-to-prepare, inexpensive dish looks like a million bucks and tastes heavenly.

1 package (10 ounces) frozen creamed spinach, thawed

1 cup vegetable broth or water

2 cups milk

$^1/_2$ cup grated Parmesan cheese

2 tablespoons chopped chives

1 teaspoon dried basil

$^1/_4$ teaspoon pepper

1 can (7 ounces) tuna fish, water-packed, drained

6 frozen patty shells (10-ounce package), defrosted

1 egg, lightly beaten

In mixing bowl or food processor, combine spinach and broth; process until smooth. Add milk, cheese, chives, basil, and pepper. Divide tuna equally among six oven-proof, $1^1/_2$-cup soup bowls. Pour soup mixture into bowls.

(cont.)

With a rolling pin, roll each patty shell into a 6-inch circle. Lay pastry on top of each bowl, leaving about a 1-inch overhang. Press the overhang firmly to the sides of the bowl.

Place the oven rack in the lower third of the oven and preheat to 400 degrees. Brush each pastry with the beaten egg.

Bake for 10 to 15 minutes or until pastry is puffed and golden brown. To eat, break up the pastry dome with a spoon and stir it into the soup. It will become thick and creamy.

Yield: 6 servings.

Each serving provides: 381 cal, 19 g pro,
5 g sat fat, 33 g unsat fat, 299 mg sodium, 25 mg chol.

Fish and Vegetable Chowder

This zesty, bone-warming bowl of cheer puts a glow on your disposition.

1^1/$_2$ pounds of fresh or frozen fish fillets (haddock or other lean white fish)

2 tablespoons butter or olive oil

^{1}/$_4$ cup chopped celery

^{1}/$_4$ cup chopped onion

^{1}/$_4$ cup whole-wheat flour

1 teaspoon herbal seasoning

^{1}/$_2$ teaspoon dried marjoram, crushed

3 cups reconstituted nonfat dry milk or low-fat milk

1 package (10 ounces) frozen mixed vegetables or one 16-ounce can mixed vegetables, drained

1 cup shredded reduced-fat, reduced-sodium mozzarella cheese (optional)

(cont.)

If fish is frozen, allow it to thaw.

Cut fillets into $3/4$-inch pieces. In a saucepan, heat the butter or oil. Add chopped celery and onion and cook till tender but not brown. Blend in the flour and seasonings. Add milk and water all at once. Cook and stir until thickened and bubbly.

Stir in the mixed vegetables. Cover and simmer for 10 minutes. Add fish pieces and shredded cheese, if you're using it. Cook about 5 minutes or till fish flakes easily and the cheese is melted.

Yield: 6 servings.

Each serving without cheese provides: 215 cal, 24 g pro,
2.1 g sat fat, 1.1 g unsat fat, 202 mg sodium, 41 mg chol.
Each serving with cheese provides: 284 cal, 28.3 g pro,
5.2 g sat fat, 3 g unsat fat, 352 mg sodium, 65 mg chol.

Tuna Cashew Casserole

Here is an old favorite that excites a nostalgic glow. It is always a favorite at jolly bring-a-dish buffets, where it never fails to get raves and requests for the recipe. Guests are always amazed to hear it's made from tuna. It tastes much more exotic.

1 can (10$^1/_2$ ounces) cream of mushroom
soup, undiluted

$^1/_4$ cup water

1 can water-packed tuna, drained

$^1/_4$ cup minced onion

1 cup diced celery

dash of pepper

1 can (3$^1/_2$ ounces) chow mein noodles
or 1 cup oat-bran crunch

$^1/_2$ cup cashew nuts

2 tablespoons oat bran

2 tablespoons wheat germ

(cont.)

Combine mushroom soup, water, tuna, onion, celery, and pepper in a 1½-quart casserole. Bake, uncovered, for 40 minutes in a 325-degree oven. Remove from oven and stir in the noodles or oat-bran crunch, nuts, and wheat germ.

To microwave: Combine all ingredients in a 2-quart casserole. Microwave on high for 5 minutes.

Yield: 6 servings.

Each serving provides: 216 cal, 8.4 g pro,
2.5 g sat fat, 8 g unsat fat, 410 mg sodium, 25 mg chol.

Aunt Betty's Fish Stroganoff

This is a delightful dish. It makes leftover fish more exotic than its original presentation. Fried green tomatoes are a lovely accompaniment. (See page 189 for recipe.) If you don't have any leftover fish, try it with 2 cans of tuna or salmon.

$1^1/_2$ to 2 cups cooked fish, flaked

1 cup sliced mushrooms

$^1/_4$ cup chopped green or red pepper

1 onion, chopped

2 cloves garlic, finely chopped

2 tablespoons butter or olive oil

1 can ($10^1/_2$ ounces) condensed tomato soup

1 cup yogurt

$^1/_2$ cup milk

1 tablespoon Worcestershire sauce

$^1/_4$ teaspoon red pepper sauce, or Tabasco®

herbal seasoning and pepper to taste

(cont.)

In a large skillet or heavy saucepan, heat the butter or oil. Add the mushrooms, pepper, onion, and garlic and sauté until tender. In a bowl, combine the soup, yogurt, milk, Worcestershire, red pepper sauce (or Tabasco®), and seasonings. Add this mixture slowly to the mushroom mixture, stirring constantly until the mixture reaches the boiling point. Add the flaked fish and serve over brown rice, noodles, or whole-grain toast.

Yield: 6 servings.

Each serving (without the noodles, rice, or toast) provides: 124 cal, 9.6 g pro, 2.5 g sat fat, 2 g unsat fat, 486 mg sodium, 30 mg chol.

Red Snapper Soup

Here's a real energy booster. Whenever I feel droopy, especially when I was pregnant, I cherish a hot bowl of this fragrant soup. I serve it for lunch on the day I make it, then freeze the remaining soup in one-bowl portions. Stop in for lunch. I'll have it hot out of the microwave for you in three minutes.

$2^1/_2$ cups vegetable stock or water

1 red snapper (about 1 pound)

1 tablespoon pickling spices

1 teaspoon herbal seasoning

1 tablespoon unsalted butter or oil

$^1/_4$ cup chopped onion

$^1/_2$ cup chopped celery

$^1/_2$ cup diced green pepper

1 cup broth or water

1 can tomato soup

$^1/_2$ cup sherry

(cont.)

Place fish in a skillet. Add 2¹/₂ cups water or stock, pickling spices, and herbal seasoning. Cover and simmer for 10 to 15 minutes. Strain the broth and reserve. Remove fish from skillet and reserve.

Heat the butter or oil in the skillet. Add the onion, celery, and pepper and lightly sauté. Add the reserved fish stock and simmer gently. Stir in the broth and tomato soup. Bone and skin the fish and add it to the soup. Stir in the sherry.

Yield: about 2 quarts or 8 servings.

Each serving provides: 123 cal, 19.5 g pro, 1.5 g sat fat,
2.9 g unsat fat, 148 mg sodium, 40 mg chol.

Brown and Crispy Salmon Cakes

These can be made with canned salmon or with leftover cooked salmon or other leftover fish. As a change from the yogurt dill sauce, try it, the second time around, with hot spaghetti sauce.

1 can (14 $^3/_4$ ounces) salmon, drained

1 tablespoon unsalted butter

$^1/_2$ cup chopped onion

$^1/_2$ cup chopped celery

1 egg, lightly beaten

$^1/_4$ cup reduced-calorie mayonnaise

juice of half a lemon

3 tablespoons chopped fresh dill

2 teaspoons dry mustard

1 teaspoon herbal seasoning

$^1/_2$ teaspoon freshly ground pepper

$^1/_4$ cup fresh bread crumbs

2 tablespoons whole-wheat pastry flour

1 tablespoon canola or olive oil

3 tablespoons chopped fresh dill

1 cup yogurt

(cont.)

Place the salmon in a mixing bowl and flake it into bite-size pieces. Break up the skin and bones and include them with the salmon.

Heat the butter and sauté the onion and celery until softened. Set aside.

In a small bowl, stir together the egg, mayonnaise, lemon juice, chopped dill, mustard, herbal seasoning, and pepper. Add this mixture, along with the bread crumbs and the onion-celery mixture, to the salmon. The mixture should be moist. Cover the mixture and refrigerate for about an hour.

On a sheet of waxed paper, spread the flour. Heat the oil in a wide, non-stick skillet. Form the fish mixture into fish cakes and carefully flour both sides of each one. Sauté the cakes over moderate heat, until they are golden, about 4 minutes. With a spatula, turn and cook the flip sides until golden, about 3 minutes. Serve with dilled yogurt (3 tablespoons chopped dill combined with 1 cup of yogurt).

Yield: 6 to 8 servings.

*Each serving (of 6) provides: 17 cal, 26 g pro, 4 g sat fat,
9 g unsat fat, 426 mg sodium, 62 mg chol.*

Salmon Cucumber Soup

1 can (7³/₄ ounces) salmon
4 small cucumbers
1 cup vegetable, fish, or chicken broth
1 medium-size onion, chopped
2 tablespoons lemon juice
¹/₂ teaspoon freshly grated pepper
1 teaspoon fresh dill, chopped, or ¹/₂ teaspoon dried dill
1 cup yogurt
toasted sesame seeds
paprika

Flake the salmon. Peel the cucumbers if they have been waxed, and cut them in chunks. Place salmon with its liquid, cucumbers, and onion in food processor or blender. Process until smooth. Add broth, lemon juice, pepper, and dill. Puree thoroughly. Stir in the yogurt. Chill.

Serve in chilled bowls. Garnish with toasted sesame seeds and paprika.

Yield: 4 to 6 servings.

Each serving (of 4) provides: 100 cal, 9 g pro, 1.1 g sat fat, .5 g unsat fat, 8 mg sodium, 0 mg chol.

CHAPTER 4
THE LEAN FAMILY:

*Tilapia, Sole, Flounder, Haddock, Halibut,
Scrod, Orange Roughy, Red Snapper,
Cod, Perch, Bass, Tile, Pollack, Grouper*

All fish are not created equal. Some are fat (over 6 percent fat content), providing about 150 calories in 3$^1/_2$ ounces. Some are moderately fat (2 to 6 percent fat), with about 114 calories in 3$^1/_2$ ounces. And some are lean (under 2 percent fat), providing about 82 calories in 3$^1/_2$ ounces. The lean family outnumbers its fattier cousins, and includes: black sea bass, cod, croaker, flounder, fluke, gray sole, grouper, haddock, halibut, lemon sole, lingcod, perch, pollack, red snapper, rockfish, scrod, skate, and tilefish. Lean fish can be prepared by any method of cooking. However, when broiling or baking it, the lean fish usually needs a little more butter, oil, or other moistener to prevent its drying out.

CREATIVE LEFTOVERS

I like to prepare more fish than I need for dinner because the leftover cooked fish is so tasty and so versatile. Try serving it with a cocktail sauce made from equal amounts of ketchup and horseradish and it tastes like a shrimp cocktail. Serve it with hot, melted butter as a dipping sauce and it tastes like lobster. In fact, this dish is called Poor Man's Lobster. A more elegant version, described below, is called Mock Lobster à la Newburgh.

The fish specified in the following recipes are the ones I used in testing the recipes. However, any member of the lean family may be substituted for the one indicated.

Simply Broiled Haddock

Halibut is the most popular fish in the market, says Paul Heckenberger, who presides over a very lively fish market in my hometown, Allentown, Pennsylvania. Haddock is Paul's favorite, too, and this is his favorite way to prepare it.

1 pound of haddock fillets

1 tablespoon melted butter

1 tablespoon lemon juice

$1/_2$ cup seasoned whole-wheat flour or bread crumbs

1 teaspoon paprika

Brush the fillets with a mixture of the butter and lemon juice. Dust with the flour or bread crumbs mixed with the paprika. Place in a baking dish greased with butter or oil or sprayed with nonfat cooking spray. Place in oven heated to 400 degrees, about 4 inches from the heat for 8 to 12 minutes, or until opaque throughout.

Yield: 4 servings.

Each serving provides: 180 cal, 22 g pro, 1 g sat fat, 1.5 g unsat fat, 60 mg sodium, 65 mg chol.

Broiled Haddock Fillets
with Fresh Grapefruit

This is a feast for the eyes, the taste buds, and the body—providing protein, vitamins, and minerals in the fish, high bioflavonoid and vitamin C in the grapefruit, and fiber in the bread cubes.

$1^1/_2$ pounds haddock fillets

1 teaspoon herbal seasoning

$^1/_8$ teaspoon freshly ground pepper

$^3/_4$ cup small bread cubes (preferably whole grain)

2 tablespoons olive or canola oil or melted butter

$^1/_2$ teaspoon dried thyme

12 fresh grapefruit sections

Wipe the fillets with a damp cloth. Sprinkle both sides with the herbal seasoner and pepper. Place in a shallow buttered or oiled baking pan.

Mix the bread cubes with 1 tablespoon of the butter or oil and the thyme. Sprinkle the cubes over the fish. Top with grapefruit sections. Brush with the remaining butter or oil. Place under broiler with oven set to 400 degrees. Broil for 10 minutes or until fish is flaky and crumbs are brown.

Yield: 6 servings.

Each serving provides: 143 cal, 24.4 g pro, 1.4 g sat fat, 3.4 g unsat fat, 62 mg sodium, 65 mg chol.

Baked Stuffed Haddock Fillets

Here is a very special high-fiber presentation to glamorize any member of the lean-fish family.

2 fillets of haddock (about 1^1/$_2$ pounds)
2 tablespoons lemon juice
^{1}/$_2$ cup fresh bread crumbs
2 tablespoons wheat bran
2 tablespoons oat bran
^{2}/$_3$ cup low-fat milk
2 tablespoons melted butter
1 cup sliced mushrooms
^{1}/$_2$ teaspoon herbal seasoning
^{1}/$_4$ teaspoon freshly ground pepper

(cont.)

Place one fillet in a baking dish greased with butter, oil, or cooking spray.

Combine bread crumbs, wheat germ, oat bran, and melted butter. Reserve half of the bread-crumb mixture. Add the chopped mushrooms, mixed with the vegetable seasoning and pepper, to the remaining crumb mixture. Place this mushroom mixture on the fillet in the baking dish. Cover with the other fillet. Pour milk over the top.

Preheat oven to 450 degrees. Brown the fish for about 5 minutes. Reduce heat to 350 degrees and bake for 25 minutes, basting with pan juices. Sprinkle with reserved crumbs and bake until crumbs are brown.

Yield: 6 servings.

Each serving provides: 171.5 cal, 20.7 g pro, 3 g sat fat, 2 g unsat fat, 176 mg sodium, 65 mg chol.

Mock Lobster à la Newburgh

This is a very special dish. Reserve it for great occasions.

2 pounds haddock fillets
2 tablespoons butter
2 tablespoons flour
1 teaspoon herbal seasoning
1 teaspoon paprika
$^1/_2$ cup low-fat milk
$^1/_2$ cup whole milk or light cream
3 egg yolks, beaten
3 tablespoons dry white wine
2 teaspoons lemon juice

Poach the fish in very little water or steam it in a steamer, strainer, or colander over boiling water. Don't let the water touch the fish. Steam for 10 minutes. Let the fish cool, then flake it.

(cont.)

In the top part of a double-boiler, melt the butter. Blend in the flour. Combine the milks and add all at once. Cook and stir until thick and bubbly. Place over hot water in the bottom part of the double-boiler. Stir a few tablespoons of the mixture into the beaten egg yolks. Return to the hot mixture. Cook, stirring constantly, until thickened. Add the flaked fish and heat through. Stir in the wine, lemon juice, and herbal seasoning. Sprinkle with paprika. Serve over cooked brown rice, in patty shells or on toast.

Yield: 6 to 8 servings.

Each serving (of 8) of the fish mixture provides: 142 cal, 20.6 g pro, 2 g sat fat, 1.15 g unsat fat, 80 mg sodium, 178 mg chol.

Louisiana Halibut

A flat fish, halibut is firm, lean, and white—thicker and more moist than the other flat fish. It is sweet and delicious whether it is grilled, baked, or poached and combines well with many different sauces. It is available as fillets or steaks. In this Louisiana version, a halibut steak is baked with onions and green peppers, which add important fiber and vitamin C. The tomato soup provides lots of vitamin A, which is a boon to your eyes, your complexion, and your ability to resist infections. This is a very wholesome and tasty dish and very easy to prepare.

1 pound halibut steak

1 large green pepper, chopped

1 large onion, chopped

1 can (10 ounces) tomato soup

1 teaspoon herbal seasoning

$^1/_4$ teaspoon freshly ground pepper, or to taste

(cont.)

Place the halibut steak in a baking dish that has been greased
with butter, oil, or cooking spray. Sprinkle with the herbal seasoning and the pepper. Combine the peppers, onions, and
tomato soup. Pour this mixture over the fish. Bake in a 350-
degree conventional oven for 20 to 25 minutes, or until it is
opaque clear through; or in your microwave oven on high for 5
to 8 minutes.

Yield: 4 servings.

*Each serving provides: 178 cal, 22.5 g pro, 0 g sat fat,
1.6 g unsat fat, 655 mg sodium, 49 mg chol.*

Note: If you wish to use this method of preparation for fillet of halibut or any member of the lean flatfish family, reduce
the baking time in the conventional oven to 20 minutes, then
check for doneness. If you're using the microwave oven, reduce
the time to 5 minutes, then check.

Peasant-Style Fish Steaks in Garlic and Wine

The onions and garlic in this flavorful dish provide a goodly amount of allicin, a substance that has been shown to inhibit the formation of blood clots.

4 large cloves fresh garlic, minced

1 tablespoon lemon juice

2 pounds halibut or other white-fish steaks

1 teaspoon herbal seasoning

$1/2$ teaspoon paprika

$1/4$ teaspoon white pepper, or to taste

1 tablespoon olive or canola oil

$1/2$ tablespoon butter

6 thin tomato slices

6 thin onion slices

6 thin green pepper slices

$1/4$ cup white wine vinegar

2 tablespoons water

$1/4$ teaspoon dried dill

parsley

(cont.)

Combine 1 clove of minced garlic with lemon juice. Set aside. Combine herbal seasoning, paprika, and pepper. Sprinkle this mixture over the fish steaks.

In a skillet, brown one side of the fish steaks in the heated oil and butter. Turn the fish over and discard any excess fat in the pan. Spread the top of each steak with the garlic mixture. Top with tomato, onion, and pepper slices. Cover the skillet and cook until fish flakes easily with a fork—about 10 to 15 minutes, depending on the thickness of the steaks.

Remove the fish and vegetables to a heated serving platter. To the skillet, add the vinegar, water, dill, and remaining 3 cloves of minced garlic. Bring to a boil, reduce heat, and simmer 2 or 3 minutes. Pour this sauce over the fish. Garnish with parsley. Serve hot or cold. It's excellent either way.

Yield: 6 servings.

Each serving provides: 245 cal, 45 g pro, 3 g sat fat,
12 g unsat fat, 207 mg sodium, 52 mg chol.

Fillet of Sole Poached
in Pineapple and Grape Juice

Whether you use flounder, Dover sole, or any light-fleshed lean fish, this is an elegantly delicious presentation, rich in fiber, vitamin C, and important minerals and enzymes. Orange or apricot juice may be substituted for the grape juice.

1 cup white grape juice

$^1/_2$ cup unsweetened pineapple juice

2 teaspoons lemon juice

$^1/_2$ teaspoon ground ginger

2 pounds fillet of sole

1 cup unsweetened pineapple chunks

$^1/_2$ cup sliced almonds, lightly toasted

In a large skillet, bring to a boil the grape juice, pineapple juice, lemon juice, and ginger. Add the fish, lower the heat, and poach the fish until it flakes—about 7 minutes.

To avoid breaking the fish, use two spatulas to remove it from the poaching liquid. Garnish with pineapple chunks and toasted almonds.

Yield: 6 servings.

Each serving provides: 221.3 cal, 24.56 g pro, 1 g sat fat,
11 g unsat fat, 58 mg sodium, 59 mg chol.

Exotic Fish Fillet Stir-Fry

Enjoy the essence of Hawaii in this lovely quick-and-easy dish that delights the taste buds with its satisfying blend of sweet and tart.

1 can (20 ounces) unsweetened pineapple chunks
2 pounds halibut, flounder, sole, haddock, or scrod
2 tablespoons butter
1 teaspoon minced garlic
2 teaspoons curry powder
1 teaspoon herbal seasoning
1 large cucumber, thinly sliced
$1/2$ cup chopped green onions
2 tablespoons lemon juice
2 teaspoons arrowroot or cornstarch
3 cups hot cooked brown rice
flaked unsweetened coconut (optional)

Drain the pineapple and reserve $1/2$ cup of the juice. Cut the fish in bite-size pieces. In a large skillet, melt the butter. Add the garlic and sauté for 1 minute. Stir in the curry powder and cook until frothy. Add the fish and the herbal seasoning. Cook over medium heat for 4 minutes. Add cucumber and onions. Cook

1 minute. Stir in pineapple, lemon juice, and the reserved pine-apple juice.

Mix arrowroot or cornstarch with 2 teaspoons of water. Stir into the fish mixture and cook until thickened—2 to 3 minutes. Serve over rice and top with coconut, if desired.

Yield: 6 servings.

Each serving, including the rice, provides: 171 cal,
5.2 g pro, 2 g sat fat, 1.2 g unsat fat, 91 mg sodium, 22 mg chol.

Sole Almondine

Tell them you're having sole almondine and the children will turn off the TV and bounce into the kitchen. No leftovers! If you don't have any children to gobble it up, the leftovers make a lovely cold salad for the next day's lunch.

1^1/$_2$ pounds sole fillets
^{1}/$_2$ cup whole-wheat pastry flour
1 teaspoon herbal seasoning
^{1}/$_2$ teaspoon freshly grated pepper
^{1}/$_3$ cup milk
2 tablespoons canola or olive oil
2 tablespoons butter
2 tablespoons lemon juice
2 tablespoons sliced almonds

Cut fillets in six serving portions. Pat dry on paper towels. On wax paper, combine flour, herbal seasoning, and pepper. Dip fish pieces first into the milk, then into the flour mixture. In a large skillet, heat oil and butter.

Cook the fillets 6 to 8 minutes or until golden brown, turning once during cooking. Remove the fish and keep it warm. Pour the fat out of the skillet. Add the almonds and the lemon juice. Cook for about 30 seconds, then pour this mixture over the fish.

Yield: 6 servings.

Each serving provides: 280 cal, 30 g pro, 5 g sat fat,
6 g unsat fat, 80 mg sodium, 80 mg chol.

Curried Flounder with Sweet Potatoes, Bananas, and Coconut

Serve this most unusual presentation on your favorite person's birthday. The sweet potatoes are an excellent source of the antioxidant beta-carotene that has been shown to not only retard the development of malignancies but also to reduce the incidence of myocardial infarction, stroke, and other adverse cardiovascular events among men with coronary disease. Bananas are a wonderful source of the potassium so important to your heart muscle. Together with the wonderful nutrients provided by the fish, this dish implies a wish for good health and a long, sweet life.

2 cups orange juice

$1/2$ teaspoon ground cinnamon

$1/4$ teaspoon ground ginger

1 teaspoon curry powder, or to taste

$1/4$ cup raisins

4 medium-size sweet potatoes, scrubbed and
cut into $1/2$-inch slices

2 pounds flounder or haddock fillets

1 large banana, peeled, sliced, and dipped in acidulated water
*(To make acidulated water, mix 1 tablespoon lemon juice or white
vinegar with 1 quart water.)*

$1/2$ cup grated unsweetened coconut, or toasted sunflower seeds

In a large, heavy pot, heat the orange juice to a boil. Add cinnamon, ginger, curry powder, raisins, and potatoes. Reduce heat to simmer, cover, and cook until potatoes are barely fork-tender, about 15 minutes. Push potatoes aside and add the fish fillets. The fish should be covered by the juice. If not, add more juice. Cover and simmer until the fish flakes, about 8 to 10 minutes.

Remove fish and potatoes to a heated platter. Spoon some liquid over all. Garnish with banana and sprinkle with coconut or toasted sunflower seeds. Serve the remaining juice on the side.

Yield: 6 servings.

Each serving provides: 338 cal, 20.7 g pro,
4.48 g sat fat, .6 g unsat fat, 82.75 mg sodium, 65 mg chol.

Egg–Battered Fillets with Walnuts

These are easy, quick, and delicious, and light as a cloud. I
like to serve them with an eggplant and banana dish, providing
a whole spectrum of complementary nutrients. This recipe
makes a little fish go a long way.

1 pound fresh or defrosted frozen scrod fillets, or any fish
in the lean family

2 eggs

$1/_2$ teaspoon herbal seasoning

1 tablespoon arrowroot or cornstarch

1 tablespoon canola or olive oil

1 tablespoon unsalted butter

2 green onions including tops, sliced or chopped

$1/_2$ cup coarsely chopped walnuts

2 teaspoons lemon juice or sherry

$1^1/_2$ tablespoons water

$1/_4$ teaspoon paprika

If the fillets are thick, slice them horizontally, $1/_2$ inch thick.
Cut the fish into $1^1/_2$-inch squares. In a small bowl, beat eggs
with the herbal seasoning. Add starch and beat well, preferably
with a wire whisk. Add the fish to the egg mixture, turning to
coat fish thoroughly.

In a large skillet, heat the oil, then add the butter. With a slotted spoon, remove the fish from the egg mixture and sauté without stirring until delicately browned. With a spatula, turn the fish and cook for another minute.

While fish is cooking, add onion, walnuts, sherry or lemon juice, water, and paprika to the leftover egg mixture. Pour this mixture over the fish, cover with lid, turn heat to medium-low, and cook until egg is set and fish is tender.

Yield: 4 servings.

Each serving provides: 202 cal, 9.6 g pro, 3.2 g sat fat,
27 g unsat fat, 30 mg sodium, 16 mg chol.

Braided Orange Roughy

From the appearance and mild flavor of the lean, low-calorie fillets you've been enjoying, you would hardly suspect that the parent fish that swims around in the coastal waters of New Zealand is frightening to look upon. It gets its name from its orange spiny coat and the bony ridges on its large head. The fish is flash-frozen as soon as it leaves the water and is still frozen when it reaches our shores and is displayed in the fish markets. Because orange roughy has so little fat, it tends to be dry, and is best when prepared with a moist companion like tomatoes or other vegetables, or with fruits that will contribute moisture. Any recipe for a lean white fish such as cod, scrod, flounder, bass, haddock, or grouper would be fine for roughy, and vice versa. (This unusual presentation gives the fillets more body and more moisture.)

1 tablespoon unsalted butter

1 large onion, chopped

1 green or red pepper, chopped

2 tomatoes chopped, or 1 cup canned tomatoes, drained

1 teaspoon herbal seasoning

$^1/_2$ teaspoon freshly ground pepper

3 orange roughy fillets (about $1^1/_2$ pounds)

2 tablespoons lemon juice

1 teaspoon paprika

In a large skillet, heat the butter and lightly sauté the onion, pepper, and tomatoes. Blend in the herbal seasoning and pepper. On a sheet of wax paper, slice the fillets lengthwise in 3 pieces each. Braid. Place the braids in an oven-proof oblong casserole. Arrange the sautéed vegetables on top and around the fish. Sprinkle with lemon juice and dust with paprika.

Bake in a 350-degree oven for 6 to 8 minutes or until fish is no longer translucent and flakes easily with a fork.

Yield: 6 servings.

*Each serving provides: 125 cal, 17 g pro, 1.07 g sat fat,
.7 g unsat fat, 76 mg sodium, 44 mg chol.*

Boxford Sole in Cream Sauce with Asparagus and Mushrooms

This tastes like pure indulgence! You can use any firm white fish, such as orange roughy, cod, scrod, haddock, halibut—whatever is available. Asparagus, frequently used as a diuretic and long considered an aphrodisiac, is a good source of potassium, zinc, and also rutin, which toughens the walls of the blood vessels, thus helping to prevent dangerous ruptures. Put POW! in your sex life and enjoy your dinner.

1 pound sole fillets or any firm white fish

$^1/_2$ cup dry white wine

$^1/_2$ teaspoon herbal seasoning

1 cup cooked asparagus, cut in segments and drained

$^1/_2$ cup cherry tomato halves

$^1/_2$ cup sliced mushrooms

2 tablespoons unsalted butter

2 tablespoons whole-wheat flour

$^1/_2$ teaspoon pepper, or to taste

$1^1/_4$ cups low-fat milk

1 egg yolk, lightly beaten

$^1/_4$ cup dry white wine

1 cup soft bread crumbs, preferably whole grain

$^1/_4$ cup grated Parmesan cheese

Poach the fish in ¹/₂ cup wine in a skillet, covered for 2 to 3 minutes or until fish flakes easily when pierced with a fork. Drain the poached fish and arrange it in a single layer in an oven-proof casserole. Sprinkle with the herbal seasoning. Top with asparagus, tomatoes, and mushrooms.

In a saucepan, melt the butter, then blend in the flour. Gradually stir in the milk, and cook, stirring, until sauce is smooth and thick. Stir a small amount of this sauce into the egg yolk, then return the egg-mixture sauce to the pot. Cook and stir until mixture comes just to the boil. Remove from heat and stir in ¹/₄ cup wine. Pour sauce over the fillets. Top with bread crumbs combined with the cheese. Bake at 350 degrees about 15 minutes.

Yield: 4 servings.

*Each serving provides: 295 cal, 37 g pro, 5 g sat fat,
5 g unsat fat, 116 mg sodium, 50 mg chol.*

Fish Stock

Keep a supply of this in your freezer. It will enhance the flavor of many dishes. It can be used to replace water or white wine where these fluids are called for.

3 pounds meaty fish bones, preferably
with head and tail on, but gills removed
(Ask your friendly fishmonger to save them for you.)

6 cups water

1 cup dry white wine

1 cup coarsely chopped onion

4 sprigs parsley

1 cup coarsely chopped celery

1 bay leaf

$1/2$ teaspoon dried thyme

6 peppercorns

herbal seasoning to taste

$1/2$ cup chopped green part of leeks (optional)

Combine all the ingredients in a large saucepan. Bring to a boil and simmer for 20 minutes. Strain. Discard the bones. (I like to bury them in the garden. The tomato plants there love them.) The fish scraps can be made to make a salad or fish cakes.

Easy-Broiled Cod

Flounder, sole, scrod, or any other lean fish can be substituted for the cod. This is quick and easy and extremely low in calories.

4 fish fillets (about 1¹/₄ pounds)
herbal seasoning and freshly ground pepper, to taste
2 tablespoons butter
1 tablespoon fine fresh bread crumbs
(preferably whole grain)
1 tablespoon sesame seeds

Preheat the broiler to high. Sprinkle the fish with herbal seasoning and pepper. Set aside.

In an oven-proof casserole large enough to hold the fish in one layer, add the butter and heat under the broiler until butter melts. Add the fish fillets and turn them over to coat both sides with butter. Combine the bread crumbs and sesame seeds. Sprinkle the fish evenly with this mixture.

Place the coated fish under the broiler about 5 inches from the source of heat. The thickness of the fish will determine the cooking time. A very thin fillet such as that of a small sole or flounder will cook in about 2 to 4 minutes. A one-inch-thick cod will need about 8 minutes.

Yield: 4 servings.

Each serving provides: 168 cal, 18 g pro, 4 g sat fat,
3 g unsat fat, 58 mg sodium, 50 mg chol.

Zesty Baked Halibut in Mustard Sauce

2 pounds halibut steak

2 tablespoons butter

2 tablespoons whole-wheat pastry flour

1 cup milk

2 teaspoons prepared mustard

1 tablespoon canola or olive oil

4 medium-size onions, sliced

1 teaspoon herbal seasoning

$1/4$ teaspoon freshly ground pepper

1 quart boiling water acidulated with
1 tablespoon lemon juice or white vinegar

In a saucepan or skillet, melt 2 tablespoons of butter, add the flour, and blend with a fork or whisk. Slowly add the milk while cooking on low heat, until the mixture thickens. Add the mustard, herbal seasoning, and pepper.

In another saucepan or skillet, heat the oil and cook the onion slices until golden and transparent.

Slip the halibut into the boiling acidulated water and simmer for 3 minutes. Drain and set aside.

In a shallow baking dish, spread the cooked onions; place the drained halibut on top of the onions. Pour the mustard sauce over all. Bake about 20 minutes at 425 degrees.

Yield: 6 servings.

Each serving provides: 190 cal, 22.8 g pro,
2.5 g sat fat, 3.2 g unsat fat, 84 mg sodium, 50 mg chol.

Red Snapper Fillets with Potatoes and Tomato-Chili Sauce

Serve with a crisp green salad and you've got a wholesome, satisfying meal!

3 pounds red snapper fillets (cod or
other firm fish fillets may be substituted)

$1/_2$ teaspoon dried oregano

$1/_4$ cup lemon juice

16 small potatoes, steamed

$1^1/_2$ cups Tomato-Chili Sauce (recipe follows)

$1/_2$ cup sliced almonds or sunflower seeds

In an oven-proof baking dish, arrange fish in a single layer. Sprinkle with oregano and lemon juice, cover tightly, and bake at 350 degrees for 5 to 10 minutes, depending on the thickness of the fish.

When fish is no longer translucent and flakes easily with the tines of a fork, place it on a heated platter. Arrange the potatoes around the fish. Cover with the Tomato-Chili Sauce. Sprinkle with sliced almonds or sunflower seeds.

TOMATO-CHILI SAUCE

2 cups tomatoes, coarsely chopped
1 tablespoon canola or olive oil
$^1/_8$ teaspoon cinnamon
$^1/_8$ teaspoon ground cloves
3 jalapeno or green chilis, chopped

In a saucepan, combine the tomatoes and oil. Cook for 5 minutes. Add remaining ingredients and simmer for 5 more minutes.

Yield: 6 servings.

Each serving, with sauce, provides: 210 cal, 20 g pro, 0 g sat fat,
2 g unsat fat, 230 mg sodium, 40 mg chol.

Halibut Balls (Gefilte Fish)

One time when we were fishing off my brother's boat, one of our kids threw his line in and said, "I hope I can catch a gefilte fish." Of course he didn't, but whatever fish he hooked could be made into gefilte fish. The word "gefilte" means stuffed. Originally, the preparation described here was intended as a stuffing, usually for carp or pike. The original purpose was to make a little fish go a long way. But, because of its unique taste appeal, gefilte fish has become a staple in Jewish cuisine, especially for Sabbath and holiday meals. Various kinds of fish may be included in the mixture, but haddock or halibut gives the fish a firm texture. Don't forget the horseradish.

2 pounds halibut or haddock,
or a combination, skin and bones removed

1 medium-size onion

2 eggs

3 tablespoons wheat germ or oat bran or a combination

$1/2$ cup fish stock or water

herbal seasoning and pepper to taste

1 large onion, sliced

1 large carrot, sliced

Put fish and onion through a food grinder or in the food processor, using the steel blade. Process until ingredients are well chopped, but not pureed. Add the eggs, wheat germ or oat bran, fish stock or water, and seasonings and process till ingredients are well blended.

Place the sliced onion and carrot in the bottom of a large pot or soup kettle. With moistened hands, form the fish mixture into "golf balls" and place them in the pot. Add fish stock or water to cover the fish. Cover pot and cook over low heat for about 1½ hours or until fish balls are tender.

Yield: 12 servings.

Each serving provides: 108 cal, 17.4 g pro, .2 g sat fat,
7.2 g unsat fat, 94 mg sodium, 97 mg chol.

Crunchy Pecan Fish Fillets

A royal dish, you can prepare this when you get home from the office and have it ready for an early dinner for family or special guests. Pecans, with their high content of iron, magnesium, potassium, vitamins A, C, and E, and polyunsaturated fats, contribute to your zest for living. I prefer grinding the nuts myself to the purchased crumbs, which very often are rancid.

2 tablespoons milk

3 tablespoons prepared mustard

4 fish fillets (especially good with scrod, haddock, or orange roughy)

1 cup ground pecans

In a small bowl, combine milk and mustard. Dip the fillets into this mixture, then into the ground pecans. Shake off excess. Place on a baking sheet, greased with butter or sprayed with non-stick cooking spray, and bake at 500 degrees for 10 to 12 minutes, or until fish flakes easily.

Yield: 4 servings.

Each serving provides: 281.5 cal, 23.4 g pro, 1.5 g sat fat, 16.2 g unsat fat, 188 mg sodium, 47 mg chol.

Broiled Fish Kabobs

Who needs hot dogs? Enjoy this marvelous picnic dish for backyard or patio entertaining. Try cooking the corn, unhusked, in the microwave for about 10 minutes. Cool and husk 6 fish fillets (try perch, bass, tile, or halibut). Corn provides vitamin A, potassium, magnesium, some vitamin C—and the lovely taste of summer.

6 fish fillets

3 cobs of corn, cooked

2 red peppers, cut into 2-inch pieces

3 tablespoons canola or olive oil

3 tablespoons low-sodium soy sauce

$^1/_2$ cup finely chopped onion

$^1/_3$ cup lemon juice

2 cloves garlic, minced

$^1/_4$ teaspoon Tabasco® sauce

1 cup whole-grain bread crumbs

1 teaspoon herbal seasoning

1 lemon or lime, cut in wedges

cooked brown or wild rice, or a combination

(cont.)

Cut fish into 2-inch pieces. Cut each ear of corn into 4 pieces. In a large shallow bowl, combine fish, corn, red pepper, oil, soy sauce, lemon juice, garlic, and Tabasco®. Mix well. Cover and refrigerate at least an hour, stirring occasionally.

When ready to serve, preheat the broiler. Drain the fish and vegetables. Reserve the marinade. Roll the fish pieces in the bread crumbs. Thread the fish, vegetables, and lemon or lime wedges, alternating, on 6 skewers about 16 inches long. Place the skewers on a greased broiler pan about 10 inches from the source of heat. Broil for 8 to 10 minutes, turning skewers and basting with the marinade, until fish flakes easily. Serve the kabobs over the rice.

Yield: 6 servings.

Each serving, with $^1/_2$ cup brown rice, provides: 368 cal,
29 g pro, 1 g sat fat, 6 g unsat fat, 366 mg sodium, 47 mg chol.

Black Sea Bass Fillets

The firm, white juicy black sea bass is not a stranger to you if you ever ordered steamed fish at a Chinese restaurant. Remember how delectable it was? You can enjoy this lean delicacy (only 2 percent fat) at home on a bed of succulent vegetables and spices. On the West Coast, black sea bass changes its name to rockfish and may even change its color to shades ranging from green to orange to red. Because black sea bass is seasonal, it's not always available at the fish market. Red snapper fillets are a good substitute.

1 tablespoon olive or canola oil

$1/2$ cup chopped onion

2 cloves garlic, minced

1 cup finely chopped leeks

1 cup chopped ripe tomatoes

$1/2$ cup finely chopped celery or fennel

1 teaspoon turmeric

$1/2$ cup dry white wine

1 cup fish broth

1 bay leaf

4 sprigs fresh thyme or 1 teaspoon dried

$1/8$ teaspoon cayenne pepper

1 teaspoon herbal seasoning

$1/8$ teaspoon freshly ground pepper

6 black sea bass fillets (about $2^{1}/_{4}$ pounds)

3 tablespoons chopped coriander or parsley

(cont.)

In a saucepan, heat the oil. Add the onion, garlic, tomatoes, celery or fennel, and turmeric. Cook, stirring over medium heat, for about 3 minutes, or until vegetables are wilted. Add the wine, fish broth, bay leaf, thyme, cayenne pepper, vegetable seasoning, and pepper. Bring to a boil and simmer 10 minutes.

In a large skillet arrange the fillets in one layer. Remove the bay leaf from the tomato sauce and pour the sauce over the fish. Cover and simmer for about 5 minutes, or until it flakes easily. Sprinkle with parsley.

Yield: 6 servings.

Each serving provides: 177.5 cal, 19.3 g pro, .3 g sat fat,
4 g unsat fat, 92 mg sodium, 41 mg chol.

Pollack in Cream

Pollack is a first cousin to cod and haddock. It tastes like its cousins but is a more substantial member of the family; the flesh of pollack is firmer and more chewy. However, it may be substituted for haddock or cod and vice versa. In this recipe the pollack is baked in cream, which makes a luscious sauce. You can use some of the sauce on your baked potato and eliminate the butter, or you can substitute milk for the cream.

$1^1/_2$ pounds fillet of pollack

2 tablespoons lemon juice

1 teaspoon prepared mustard

$^1/_2$ teaspoon Worcestershire sauce

1 teaspoon herbal seasoning

$^1/_4$ teaspoon freshly ground pepper

3 small onions, quartered

1 cup light cream

parsley and paprika

Wipe the fish with a damp cloth and place in an oven-proof

(cont.)

casserole. Combine the lemon juice, mustard, Worcestershire sauce, herbal seasoning, and pepper. Pour this mixture over the fish. Add the onions and the cream.

Bake in a 400-degree oven for about 15 minutes, or until fish flakes easily. Garnish with parsley and sprinkle with paprika.

Yield: 6 servings.

Each serving provides: 214 cal, 20.9 g pro,
7 g sat fat, 7.1 g unsat fat, 75 mg sodium, 50 mg chol.

Butter-Broiled Snapper

A snap to prepare, it has a delectable, succulent flavor.

$1^1/_2$ pounds snapper fillets
2 tablespoons unsalted butter, melted
$^1/_4$ cup lemon juice
$^1/_2$ cup whole-grain bread crumbs
1 teaspoon herbal seasoning
$^1/_4$ teaspoon freshly ground pepper

Brush the fish with the butter and lemon juice. Coat the fish with the bread crumbs combined with the herbal seasoning and pepper. Broil for 5 to 8 minutes, or until fish flakes easily with a fork.

Yield: 6 servings.

Each serving provides: 180 cal, 21 g pro, 6 g sat fat,
5.6 g unsat fat, 126 mg sodium, 40 mg chol.

Beautiful Baked Fish Fillets

1 pound fish fillets (flounder, sole, etc.)
1 cup plain yogurt
2 tablespoons finely chopped onion
2 tablespoons finely chopped green or red pepper
2 tablespoons chopped dill pickle
1 tablespoon chopped parsley
1 tablespoon lemon juice
$1/4$ teaspoon dry mustard
paprika
lemon slices
1 ripe avocado, pitted, peeled, and sliced

Arrange fish in a baking dish. In a small mixing bowl, combine yogurt, onion, pepper, pickle, parsley, lemon juice, and mustard. Spread the yogurt mixture over the fish. Sprinkle with paprika. Bake at 375 degrees for about 15 minutes, or until fish flakes easily. Garnish with lemon slices and avocado slices.

Yield: 4 servings.

Each serving provides: 192 cal, 23.9 g pro, 3.6 g sat fat, 9.9 g unsat fat, 89 mg sodium, 45 mg chol.

Baked Grouper, Mediterranean Style

The grouper, a large and low-fat fish, is known as the "Chameleon of the Sea." It not only changes its color to match its surroundings, it can actually paint its own stripes when near other, threatening fish. But even more fascinating is the sex life of the grouper. (Talk show hosts would love them.) They are all female at birth, and change their sex at a later age. They are cousins to the bass family and can be used interchangeably. A savory blend of flavors and colors is this grouper recipe, which delights the eye and the taste buds. The orange provides vitamin C, which helps you to metabolize important minerals. It is also one of the antioxidants that have been shown to retard the development of malignancies.

2 tablespoons olive oil

2 tablespoons lemon juice

1 tablespoon fresh oregano leaves or $^1/_2$ teaspoon dried

1 teaspoon finely shredded orange zest

2 pounds grouper fillets

1 teaspoon herbal seasoning

$^1/_4$ teaspoon freshly ground pepper, or to taste

thick slices of orange or orange wedges

$^1/_4$ cup small black olives (optional)

(cont.)

Heat oven to 350 degrees. In a shallow baking dish, large enough to hold the fish in a single layer, combine the oil, lemon juice, oregano, and orange zest. Place the fish fillets in the dish and turn them to coat with the oil and lemon mixture. Sprinkle with herbal seasoning and pepper.

Place in the oven and bake for 20 to 25 minutes or until the fish is opaque and tender in the center when flaked with a fork. Baste with the pan juices several times during the baking period. Garnish with the orange pieces and the olives.

Yield: 6 servings.

Each serving, with olives, provides: 166.4 cal, 19.73 g pro, .2 g sat fat, 6 g unsat fat, 341.5 mg sodium, 50 mg chol.

Tilapia

Tilapia is a warm-water fish native to the Nile and other rivers in the Middle East. Maybe you know it as St. Peter's fish. When you buy tilapia today, chances are it never came near the Middle East but was raised in heat-controlled water tanks, fed and fattened with pellets of grains, vitamins, and minerals, and then placed in clean water without food for three to five days to get rid of any offensive fishy flavor. Then it traveled to the bed of ice in your fish market. (This is aquaculture.)

Tilapia are farm-raised in Florida, California, Maryland, and Pennsylvania. The largest production sites, Solar Aqua Farms, a corporate partner of Chiquita Brands International in Sun City, California, distributes as much as 15,000 pounds a week all over the country. For those concerned with the hazards of ocean pollution, aquaculture represents safe harbor. In fact, the demand for the fish is so great that producers say they cannot keep up with it.

Tilapia promises to become the "fish of the future," not only for its safety but for its white, delicate, moist flesh, which picks up the flavors of sauce and seasoning and cooks up in less than 5 minutes.

If tilapia is not yet in your local market, ask the manager of the fish department if it can be stocked. Until it is available to you, use flounder, sole, or orange roughy in the following recipes.

Lemon-Broiled Herbed Tilapia

Have a party. Serve this recipe with lovely Almond-Acorn-Squash Bowls (halved acorn squash stuffed with cooked brown rice, raisins, and chopped toasted almonds, and baked).

2 teaspoons canola or olive oil

2 tablespoons lemon juice

1 garlic clove, crushed

$1/_8$ teaspoon dried thyme or oregano

2 tilapia fillets (3 to 6 ounces each)

pepper to taste

2 teaspoons chopped parsley

Preheat boiler.

Combine 1 teaspoon oil with lemon juice, garlic, and thyme or oregano.

If you're not using a non-stick broiler pan, line it with foil, then place the lined broiler pan 2 inches from the heat and pre-heat it for 2 to 3 minutes.

Rub one side of each fillet with oil and lay it in a heated broiling pan, oiled side down. Spoon about two-thirds of the lemon-juice mixture over the fillets and broil 5 to 10 minutes, depending on thickness of fish (an inch-thick fillet will take 10 minutes). Baste twice, using lemon-juice mixture and pan juices.

Remove from broiler, transfer to warm plates, and spoon pan juices over fillets. Sprinkle each fillet with pepper and chopped parsley.

Yield: 2 servings.

Each serving provides: 200 cal, 30 g pro,
1 g sat fat, 8 g unsat fat, 100 mg sodium, 40 mg chol.

Baked Tilapia with Sweet Spices and Tangy Dressing

You'll enjoy this lovely medley of flavors.

1 teaspoon ground ginger

$^1/_4$ teaspoon nutmeg

$^1/_4$ teaspoon cinnamon

1 teaspoon ground cumin

$^1/_4$ teaspoon cayenne pepper

2 teaspoons minced garlic

4 tilapia (about $2^1/_2$ pounds total)

2 teaspoons olive or canola oil

Orange-Onion Relish

In a small bowl, combine the ginger, nutmeg, cinnamon, cumin, cayenne, and garlic. Wash the tilapia and dry with absorbent paper. Rub the inside cavities with the spice mixture.

Arrange the fish in a shallow glass baking dish and brush with the oil. Cover lightly with foil and bake in a preheated 400-

degree oven for about 15 minutes, or until flesh is opaque when tested with a fork. Serve with Orange-Onion Relish.

Yield: 4 servings.

Each serving, without the relish dressing, provides: approximately 117 cal, 21 g pro, 1 g sat fat, 6 g unsat fat, 100 mg sodium, 50 mg chol.

ORANGE-ONION RELISH

2 medium-size oranges, peeled, seeded, and diced

$1/4$ cup red onion, finely chopped

2 tablespoons salad dressing

In a small bowl, combine oranges and onion. Stir in the salad dressing.

Yield: about 1 cup, or 4 servings.

Each serving provides: 51 cal, 1.4 g pro, practically no fat, sodium, or cholesterol.

Lightly Sautéed Garlic-Flavored Tilapia

4 tilapia fillets (3¹/₂ ounces each)
2 tablespoons lemon juice
herbal seasoning and pepper
1 teaspoon olive or canola oil
2 teaspoons butter
1 teaspoon minced garlic
1 tablespoon chopped parsley

Wash fillets and pat dry with absorbent paper. Sprinkle with lemon juice, herbal seasoning, and a little pepper.

In a large non-stick skillet, heat the oil and butter. Sauté the fish for 2 to 3 minutes on each side, or until nicely browned. Remove from the skillet and place on a heated platter.

Stir the garlic and parsley into the pan juices and heat. Spoon the garlic sauce over the fish.

Yield: 4 servings.

Each serving provides: 125 cal, 21 g pro,
1.5 g sat fat, 6 g unsat fat, 40 mg sodium, 50 mg chol.

CHAPTER 5
THE FATTER FISH
(6 to 20 percent Omega-3 Fatty Acid Content)

When a fish is called "fatty," it is not an insulting sobriquet. It means that it has a more pronounced flavor and, because it has over 6 percent fat, it is easily broiled without any additional fat. But, more important, it means that it provides more wonder-working Omega-3's than its cousins on the lean side.

When cooking fatty fish, remember that, unlike lean fish, it needs few additions to keep it moist and flavorful. A touch of flavored vinegar, lemon, lime, or orange juice enhances the flavor while it mellows the taste. The best way to preserve the Omega-3's is to broil, bake, poach, or steam the fish.

The recipes for fatty fish in this section can be used interchangeably for bluefish, butterfish, mackerel, ocean perch, pompano, salmon, shad, or tuna.

Salmon, King of Fish

If the fish of all the rivers, lakes, and oceans held a popularity contest, which one do you think would swim down the runway wearing the crown and throwing kisses? No doubt about it, salmon wins the crown. In fact, Izaak Walton, author of *The Compleat Angler,* dubbed salmon "king of fish"; indeed, on of the most popular varieties is called king salmon.

Salmon's unique rich and meaty flavor is love at first bite, no matter how you choose to serve it—poached, broiled, grilled, smoked, or baked...as steaks, fillets, whole or out of a can.

Whether it swims in the Atlantic or Pacific, salmon is high in protein and, compared to other fish, is high in fat. But even the fattest has less fat than chicken or steak, and what fat it does have is unsaturated and a superior source of the wonder-working Omega-3 fatty acids.

There are some differences between the salmon of the Atlantic and their cousins in the Pacific. Atlantic salmon is pink and comes to market fresh. Pacific salmon comes in many forms. It may come in cans, smoked or fresh, and the varieties include the prized king, also called chinook, which comes from Alaska and the Columbia River area. Other varieties from the Pacific include the red-fleshed sockeye, pinkish-silvery coho, and yellow-tinted dog (salmon which has very little fat).

Canned salmon is practically a staple in every home. Why not? It is so versatile and so good-tasting. You've probably noticed the price differential between the costly squat cans and the more economical tall cans. That's because the squat can contains the most desirable part, cut from the center, while the tall can houses the tail meat.

When using canned salmon, be sure to include the bones and skin. Simply mash them up. They are a wonderful source of calcium.

The recipes that follow will help you to enjoy the wonderful flavor and health benefits of succulent salmon.

Salmon Salad with Gingery Raisin Sauce

Serve it hold or cold as a salad on a bed of greens and shredded carrots, or serve it with a baked potato and steamed broccoli. However you serve it, dress it up with the delicious raisin sauce included in this recipe.

1 tablespoon arrowroot or cornstarch

1 cup orange juice

$^1/_2$ cup raisins

2 tablespoons sliced green onion

2 teaspoons Dijon mustard

1 teaspoon grated fresh ginger or $^1/_3$ teaspoon powdered

1 teaspoon chopped fresh dill weed

$^1/_4$ teaspoon herbal seasoning

4 salmon steaks (about $1^1/_2$ pounds)

Mix the cornstarch with 2 tablespoons of the orange juice. Add it to the remaining orange juice and bring it to a boil, stirring until thickened. Stir in the raisins, onion, mustard, ginger, dill, and herbal seasoning. Mix well and set aside.

Place the fish in a buttered baking dish. Place the oven rack about 6 inches below the source of heat. Broil for 5 to 8 minutes on each side. To test for doneness, see if you can remove the center bone without taking any of the flesh with it.

To serve as a salad, place each steak atop a bowl of salad greens and shredded carrots. Drizzle with the raisin dressing.

Yield: 4 servings.

Each serving provides: 262 cal, 20 g pro, 4.4 g fat,
5.2 g unsat fat, 53 mg sodium, 66 mg chol.

Grilled Whole Salmon
with Ginger and Lime

Salmon is a great fish for grilling, because it won't dry out too much. Make sure the grill is very clean and very hot. In lieu of a grill, you could use a double thickness of oiled foil with lots of holes punched in it, to allow the smoke to come through.

$^3/_4$ cup (6 ounces) reduced-calorie cream cheese

$^1/_2$ cup plain yogurt

1 tablespoon chopped candied ginger or ginger marmalade

grated rind of 1 lime

3- to 4-pound whole salmon, cleaned and scaled,
head and tail intact

canola or peanut oil for greasing the grill and
lubricating the fish

freshly ground pepper to taste

1 lime, sliced

about 1 teaspoon ground ginger, or to taste

To make the sauce, mix together the cheese, yogurt, candied ginger or ginger marmalade, and lime zest in a small bowl.

To grill the salmon, brush the salmon—inside and outside—with the oil. Sprinkle with pepper and ginger. Put the lime slices in the cavity of the fish. Brush the grill with oil. Place the fish on the grill. Cook for 10 minutes. Brush again with oil and, with a spatula, carefully turn it. Continue cooking for 8 to 10 minutes, or until the fish flakes easily when tested with a fork.

Using the spatula, transfer the salmon to a serving platter. Serve the hot salmon with the room-temperature lime-ginger sauce.

Yield: 6 servings.

Each serving provides: 265 cal, 23 g pro, 28 g sat fat, 19 g unsat fat, 110 mg sodium, 70 mg chol.

Broiled Marinated Salmon Steaks

Halibut, tuna, or swordfish may be substituted for the salmon in this quick-and-easy recipe.

2 tablespoons canola or olive oil

$1/_3$ cup wine or balsamic vinegar

1 teaspoon Worcestershire sauce

freshly ground pepper, to taste

1 bay leaf

2 tablespoons chopped parsley

2 tablespoons chopped fresh dill or 1 teaspoon dried

$1^1/_2$ pounds salmon cut in 1-inch-thick steaks

In a shallow bowl, combine the oil, vinegar, Worcestershire sauce, pepper, bay leaf, and parsley. Add the fish steaks. Cover and refrigerate for at least 3 hours, turning occasionally.

Remove from marinade and place on a buttered or foil-covered broiler pan. Baste with the marinade. Place the broiler pan about 3 inches from the heat source. Broil about 10 minutes, or until fish flakes easily when tested with a fork. Baste with the sauce before serving.

Yield: 6 servings.

*Each serving provides: 193 cal, 18 g pro, 1.5 g sat fat,
3.6 g unsat fat, 175 mg sodium, 58 mg chol.*

Honey and Ginger Salmon Fillet

If you have any of the honey-ginger sauce left over from the following recipe, it makes a lovely salad dressing.

1 tablespoon honey

1 tablespoon finely grated fresh ginger or $1/2$ teaspoon ground

3 tablespoons lemon juice

1 teaspoon sodium-reduced soy sauce

1 teaspoon minced parsley

$1^1/_2$ pound salmon fillet

1 teaspoon herbal seasoning

$1/4$ teaspoon freshly ground pepper, or to taste

In a small bowl, combine the honey, ginger, lemon juice, soy sauce, and parsley.

Place the salmon in an oven-proof baking dish, buttered, oiled, or sprayed with non-stick cooking spray. Spread with about half of the honey-ginger mixture. Sprinkle with herbal seasoning and pepper.

Bake in a preheated 425-degree oven for 10 minutes per inch of thickness. About halfway through the cooking period, spread over the fish the remaining honey-ginger sauce.

Yield: 6 servings.

Each serving provides: 159 cal, 21.6 g pro,
2.63 g sat fat, 3 g unsat fat, 97 mg sodium, 52 mg chol.

Poached Salmon

This is an elegant dish to set before the king. Notice that there is no fat needed in the preparation of poached fish. The court bouillon that remains in the poacher can be refrigerated or frozen and used again.

water to fill fish poacher halfway

2 cups dry white wine

2 tablespoons peppercorns

1 tablespoon herbal seasoning

2 onions, sliced

$^1/_2$ cup white wine vinegar

1 cup chopped celery with the tops included

5- to 6-pound whole salmon or one that fits your poacher

lemon slices

Place the water, wine, peppercorns, herbal seasoning, onions, vinegar, and celery in the poacher and boil for 15 minutes. Strain the mixture (it's now called a court bouillon) and let it cool to room temperature.

Wash the salmon; make sure the scales are removed; and trim off all of the fins. Check to see if the salmon fits the poacher. If it's a bit too long, trim off a little of the tail. With a ruler, measure the thickest part of the fish and take note of it. Wrap the fish in cheesecloth and place it in the poacher over high heat. When the court bouillon begins to boil, begin timing the cooking. It should cook for 10 minutes per inch of thickness. A 2-inch-thick fish should cook for 20 minutes. For every tenth of an inch more, figure another minute.

Remove the fish promptly to a warm platter. Carefully remove the cheesecloth. Serve triumphantly with a yogurt and dill sauce on the side or any of the sauces suggested in the foregoing recipes.

Yield: 10 servings.

Each serving, without the sauce, provides: 180 cal, 20 g pro, 4 g sat fat, 6.4 g unsat fat, 45 mg sodium, 66 mg chol.

YOGURT-DILL SAUCE

1 cup yogurt

1 teaspoon grated onion

3 tablespoons minced fresh dill

1 teaspoon lemon juice

In a small glass bowl, combine all ingredients.

Yield: 1 cup.

One tablespoon provides: 9.5 cal, .5 g pro, .5 g sat fat, 7 mg sodium.

Salmon Mousse

After unmolding, go creative. Use a black olive for an eye, sprigs of dill for fins, and lemon half-slices for scales. This never fails to make a hit.

1 tablespoon unflavored gelatin

$1/4$ cup cold water

$1/2$ cup boiling water

$1/2$ cup reduced-calorie mayonnaise

1 tablespoon lemon juice

$1/4$ teaspoon cayenne pepper

1 tablespoon grated onion

1 teaspoon herbal seasoning

$1/4$ teaspoon paprika

$1/4$ teaspoon nutmeg

2 cups chopped-up cooked salmon pieces
(may be leftover scraps)

$1/2$ cup heavy cream, whipped

Soften the gelatin in the cold water. Add the boiling water. Stir to dissolve gelatin, then cool. Add the mayonnaise, lemon juice, cayenne pepper, grated onion, herbal seasoning, paprika, and nutmeg. Mix well. Chill the mixture to the consistency of raw egg white. Add the chopped-up salmon pieces and mix well. This can be done in the food processor, using the steel blade. Fold the whipped cream into the salmon mixture.

Oil a fish mold. Add the salmon mixture. Refrigerate the mold until the mixture is set. Unmold on a serving platter and garnish with sprigs of dill and lemon slices. Serve with Yogurt-Dill sauce from the preceding recipe.

Yield: 8 servings.

*Each serving provides: 174 cal, 12 g pro, 4.9 g sat fat,
7 g unsat fat, 43 mg sodium, 66 mg chol.*

Grilled Salmon on a Roll

What a great dish for a patio supper or picnic! Your guests will bless you.

3 salmon steaks (each about 1 inch thick)
1 tablespoon canola or olive oil
3 tablespoons lemon juice
1 teaspoon herbal seasoning
$1/2$ teaspoon freshly ground pepper
6 sandwich rolls, preferably whole grain, cut in halves, crosswise
romaine lettuce leaves
cucumber slices

Brush both sides of the salmon steaks with the oil. Sprinkle with lemon juice, herbal seasoning, and pepper. Let them rest for 10 minutes.

Grease the grill with cooking spray or brush it with oil. Place the salmon in the center of grill over hot coals and allow to cook for 10 minutes, turning them once. On the side of the grill, lightly toast the split rolls.

Divide the salmon into 6 portions. Remove any skin and bones. Place a lettuce leaf and cucumber slices on bottom halves of the rolls. Place salmon on top and cover with the top halves.

Yield: 6 servings.

Each serving provides: 292 cal, 24.8 g pro,
4.7 g sat fat, 6 g unsat fat, 285 mg sodium, 66 mg chol.

Carolyn's Salmon-Noodle Kugel with Mushrooms

This is a tasty meal in a dish, wonderful to have on hand when unexpected guests drop in. It freezes well.

1 can (7³/₄ ounces) or 1 cup flaked leftover salmon

8-ounce package medium-size noodles, cooked

1 cup sliced mushrooms

1 tablespoon butter

3 tablespoons chopped green onion

1 cup cottage cheese

2 tablespoons wheat germ or oat bran

¹/₂ cup plain yogurt

1 tablespoon chopped dill

1 tablespoon chopped parsley

1 tablespoon sesame seeds

Flake the salmon. Cook and drain the noodles. In a large skillet, melt the butter and lightly sauté the mushrooms and onion. Stir the flour into the pan. Add the yogurt. Heat the mixture but do not allow it to boil. Add the cottage cheese, dill, and parsley.

(cont.)

Combine the cheese mixture with the salmon and cooked noodles. Place the mixture in a greased 8 x 10-inch oven-proof casserole. Bake at 350 degrees for 20 to 25 minutes in a conventional oven, or 8 to 10 minutes in the microwave.

Yield: 6 servings.

Each serving provides: 254 cal, 19 g pro,
4.3 g sat fat, 2 g unsat fat, 245 mg sodium, 80 mg chol.

Variation: Especially for the kids. Make a Salmon-Noodle Pizza. Simply top with a half-cup of grated part-skim mozzarella cheese before baking.

Salmon Soufflé

Delicately delicious, this dish provides a powerhouse of nutrients.

1 can (7³/₄ ounces) salmon or 1 cup leftover salmon

1 cup milk, including liquid from salmon

2 tablespoons butter

2 tablespoons whole-wheat flour

1 teaspoon herbal seasoning

¹/₄ teaspoon freshly ground pepper

¹/₄ teaspoon dry mustard

1 tablespoon minced parsley

3 eggs, separated

If you're using canned salmon, drain it and reserve the liquid. Add milk to the salmon liquid to total 1 cup. If you're using left-over salmon, use 1 cup milk.

In a skillet, melt the butter, blend in the flour, herbal sea-soning, pepper, and dry mustard. Add the milk mixture, and cook, stirring constantly, until thickened and smooth. Add the salmon and parsley. Beat the egg yolks. Slowly add the salmon mixture to the yolks, mixing thoroughly.

Beat egg whites stiff but not dry. Fold the egg whites gen-tly into the salmon mixture. Turn into an ungreased 1-quart soufflé dish. Bake at 350 degrees for 30 to 40 minutes, or until brown and puffy. Serve immediately.

Yield: 4 servings.
Each serving provides: 257 cal, 18.8 g pro, 7 g sat fat,
4.6 g unsat fat, 380 mg sodium, 210 mg chol.

Crispy Oven-Fried Salmon

Oven-frying is a healthy substitute for deep-fat frying. The result is a moist interior and a deliciously crunchy outside.

1 pound fish fillets (salmon or any kind)

2 tablespoons reduced-calorie mayonnaise

5 tablespoons whole-grain bread crumbs

1 teaspoon parsley flakes

$^1/_2$ teaspoon paprika

Coat fish on both sides with mayonnaise. Combine bread crumbs, parsley flakes, and paprika. Coat the fillets with this mixture. Place in a shallow glass casserole dish. Bake at 450 degrees for 12 minutes.

Yield: 4 servings.

Each serving provides: 221 cal, 21.7 g pro,
2 g sat fat, 3.6 g unsat fat, 88 mg sodium, 66 mg chol.

Shad, the Harbinger of Spring

When shad makes its appearance in the fish markets, you know it's time to put away the snow shovel and look for daffodils on the hill. Shad is a most welcome harbinger of spring. Enjoy it frequently when it's in season. It won't be around very long. It has a most delectable flavor, and comes to us from unpolluted water. It will neither swim nor spawn in polluted waters.

Because shad has an elaborate bone structure, it was considered "trash fish" for many years, before a workable system for removing those bones was devised. It is now generally available as boned fillets.

If you'd like to bake a whole shad, try the first of the following recipes.

Whole Shad

Using this method, the bones will soften but they will not disappear.

1 whole shad (about 3 pounds)

juice of 1 lemon

dry white wine, enough to cover the fish

Marinate the fish in the wine combined with the lemon juice, for several hours or overnight. Make sure the wine-lemon combo covers the fish.

To bake the fish, place it in an oven-to-table baking pan. Pour the marinade over it. Bake in a moderate oven, about 350 degrees for 10 minutes, per inch of fish, measured at its thickest point. If the fish measures $2^1/_2$ inches thickness, allow 25 minutes baking time.

Yield: 6 servings.

Each serving provides: 180 cal, 20 g pro, 3 g sat fat,
6.6 g unsat fat, 200 mg sodium, 70 mg chol.

Grilled or Broiled Marinated Herb-Flavored Shad

1 fillet of shad
1 teaspoon herbal seasoning
$1/_4$ teaspoon freshly ground pepper
2 tablespoons olive or canola oil
2 tablespoons lemon juice
$1/_2$ teaspoon finely crumbled bay leaf
1 tablespoon fresh thyme or $1/_2$ teaspoon dried
$1/_4$ teaspoon paprika
lemon or lime wedges

Place the fillet, skin side down, in a baking dish. Sprinkle with the herbal seasoning and the pepper.

In a small dish, combine the oil, lemon juice, bay leaf, and thyme and spread over and around the fish. Cover and let stand in the refrigerator for 2 hours.

Preheat the broiler to high. Spread the fish with paprika. Place under broiler about 4 inches from the source of heat and broil for 5 minutes. Cut fish in half, lengthwise. Place on hot serving dishes. Spoon a little marinade over each serving. Serve with lemon or lime wedges.

Yield: 2 servings.

Each serving provides: 190 cal, 18.6 g pro, 2 g sat fat, 12 g unsat fat, 150 mg sodium, 370 mg chol.

Baked Shad without Bones

This fish provides lots of good calcium because you eat bones and all. The bones dissolve during the long baking period. You may find some dilution of the flavor. The potatoes and onions make a very pleasant counterpoint to the flavor of the fish.

1 whole shad (about 3 pounds)

2 tablespoons vinegar

4 medium-size onions, sliced

5 medium-size potatoes, scrubbed and sliced

1 teaspoon herbal seasoning

$1/_2$ teaspoon freshly ground pepper

Cut gashes about $1/_4$ inch apart along both sides of the shad. Place the shad on a large piece of aluminum foil or parchment paper. Sprinkle the vinegar all over the fish. Surround the fish with the potatoes and onions. Sprinkle all with the herbal seasoning.

Fold and seal the foil or parchment paper and place in baking pan. Bake 6 hours in a 300-degree oven. The little bones will soften and crumble like the bones in canned salmon. Everything is edible except the backbone.

Yield: 6 to 8 servings.

Each serving (of 6), with potatoes and onions, provides: 171 cal, 22.8 g pro, 3 g sat fat, 6.6 g unsat fat, 207 mg sodium, 70 mg chol.

Shad with Tomatoes and Mushrooms

1 boneless fillet of shad
$1/2$ teaspoon herbal seasoning
$1/4$ teaspoon freshly ground pepper
$1/4$ cup milk
$1/2$ cup whole-grain flour
2 tablespoons canola or olive oil
2 cups sliced mushrooms
1 teaspoon finely minced garlic
1 tablespoon butter
$1/2$ cup canned tomatoes, crushed
2 tablespoons finely chopped parsley

(cont.)

Split fillet in half, crosswise. Sprinkle with herbal seasoning and pepper. Place in a small flat bowl with the milk. Remove fish pieces from the milk without draining. Place the dripping fish pieces in the flour and coat both sides.

Heat the oil in a skillet. Add the fish pieces, skin side up. Cook about $1^1/_2$ minutes over high heat or until golden brown. Carefully turn and continue cooking on the other side over moderately low heat for 3 to 4 minutes. Transfer the fish to two warm serving plates.

Heat the oil in the skillet and add mushrooms, herbal seasoning, and pepper. Cook, stirring, about 2 minutes. Add garlic and butter. Stir until butter melts.

In a small saucepan, heat the tomatoes and cook down for about 5 minutes. Spoon half of the tomatoes onto each piece of fish. Pour mushrooms over all, and sprinkle with parsley.

Yield: 2 servings.

Each serving provides: 400 cal, 25.5 g pro,
8 g sat fat, 14 g unsat fat, 258 mg sodium, 80 mg chol.

Shad Roe

Fish roe consists of thousands of tiny, unfertilized eggs clustered together and enclosed in two sacs. It is very rich in vitamins and minerals and low in fat. The Indians fed it to weaning babies as a nourishing substitute for mother's milk.

Shad roe is the most popular of the species, but the roe of other fish are also tasty and nourishing. Caviar is the processed roe of the sturgeon. It is very expensive and much too salty for my taste buds. But the roe of other fish—salmon, cod, pike, flounder, tuna, herring, carp, and shad—are also delectable, not nearly so expensive, and certainly less salty.

Shad roe is at its most flavorful when the eggs are small and dark red. Fresh shad roe should be firm to the touch, not soft or mushy. It can be prepared in many different ways and presents an entirely new taste sensation with each procedure.

Shad Roe in Buttery Lemon Sauce

2 pairs of shad roe

1 cup milk

$^1/_2$ cup whole-wheat flour

4 tablespoons unsalted butter

2 tablespoons olive or canola oil

1 tablespoon dry white wine

2 tablespoons chopped chives or scallions

2 tablespoons lemon juice

1 teaspoon herbal seasoning

$^1/_2$ teaspoon freshly ground pepper

lemon or lime slices for garnish

Soak the shad roe in milk for about 10 minutes. Drain and pat dry. Spread the flour on wax paper. Dredge the roe in the flour.

In a 12-inch skillet, heat 2 tablespoons butter and 2 tablespoons oil. Sauté the floured roe until golden brown, about 6 minutes on each side. Remove from the skillet and keep warm.

Add the wine to the sauce in the skillet and heat, scraping the tasty morsels from the bottom of the pan. Add chives and the remaining 2 tablespoons butter. Heat until the butter is golden brown. Stir in the lemon juice, herbal seasoning, and pepper. Pour the sauce over the shad roe. Garnish with lemon or lime slices and serve immediately.

Yield: 4 servings.

*Each serving provides: 262 cal, 15 g pro, 7.8 g sat fat,
14.9 g unsat fat, 42 mg sodium, chol N.A. (not available).*

Nancy's Shad Roe Salad

2 cups water

1 slice lemon

1 tablespoon cider vinegar

1 pair of shad roe

1 cup chopped celery

1 small cucumber, chopped and chilled

DRESSING

1 tablespoon horseradish

2 tablespoons lemon juice

$^1/_4$ cup mayonnaise

$^1/_2$ cup plain yogurt

$^1/_2$ teaspoon herbal seasoning

$^1/_4$ teaspoon freshly ground pepper

Combine the water, lemon, and vinegar in a saucepan. Add the fish roe and simmer for about 20 minutes. Remove to a wire rack to drain, then chill it in the refrigerator. After it is chilled, cut it into cubes.

To make the dressing, combine the horseradish, lemon juice, mayonnaise, yogurt, herbal seasoning, and pepper. Add the chopped celery and cucumber. Last, add the cubed shad and toss, being careful not to break up the roe.

Yield: 4 servings.

Each serving provides: 191 cal, 13.7 g pro, 2 g sat fat,
1.5 g unsat fat, 41.15 mg sodium, chol N.A. (not available).

Trout

Trout is a smallish fish, weighing in at 1 to 5 pounds. Unless you have snared your own catch, the rainbow trout you're having for dinner has been farm-raised.

A moderately fatty fish, trout is delicious whether it is steamed, broiled, baked, grilled, or sautéed. It is an excellent sauce of Omega-3 fatty acids, which have been shown to have a preventive effect against coronary heart disease.

Delight your taste buds and your heartstrings with the following recipes.

Broiled Rainbow Trout

So easy to prepare, so moist and delicious! Serve with steamed broccoli topped with chopped roasted walnuts and herbed brown rice.

4 small trout, pan-ready

$3/4$ cup low-calorie Italian dressing or your own dressing made with olive oil, vinegar, garlic, and herbs

Marinate the trout in the dressing for at least 30 minutes. Broil 4 inches from source of heat for 10 minutes per inch of thickness, measured at its thickest part.

After 5 minutes of cooking time, brush the fish with the marinade, turn and continue broiling until the fish flakes easily when tested with a fork.

Yield: 4 servings.

Each serving provides: 267 cal, 24.9 g pro,
4 g sat fat, 6.37 g unsat fat, 52 mg sodium, 50 mg chol.

Trout, Hardly Cooked

Undercooked fish is nutritionally superior—moist, sweet, and very delicious. Try this way of preparing it.

4 small trout, or as many as you have mouths to feed

$^1/_2$ cup yellow cornmeal

1 teaspoon canola or olive oil

Place the cornmeal on a sheet of wax paper. Turn the fish in the cornmeal to coat both sides.

Heat a skillet large enough to hold the fish in a single layer. Add the oil; put in the trout. Let the cornmeal brown very lightly, then turn the fish and turn off the heat. Leave the fish in the skillet just long enough to heat through but not cook. Serve at once, browned side up, with wedges of lemon.

Yield: 4 servings.

Each serving provides: 226 cal, 26 g pro, 3 g sat fat, 3.87 g unsat fat, 52 mg sodium, 50 mg chol.

Barcelona Trout Fillets

You get an intermingling of fine flavors when you cook the whole meal in one skillet.

1 teaspoon olive or canola oil

1 cup brown rice

$1/_2$ cup minced celery

$1/_2$ cup minced onion

$1/_3$ cup chopped parsley

3 cloves garlic, minced

1 tablespoon fresh thyme or $1/_2$ teaspoon dried

2 cups vegetable or fish stock, or water

1 pound trout fillets

3 chopped plum tomatoes or $1/_2$ cup canned tomatoes

$1/_2$ cup green peas or mung bean sprouts

In a large skillet, heat the oil. Add the rice, celery, onion, parsley, garlic, paprika, and thyme. Sauté for 3 to 4 minutes, stirring constantly. Add the stock. Bring to a boil, then reduce heat. Cover and simmer for 25 minutes.

Add the fillets and simmer for 8 more minutes. Add the tomatoes and peas or sprouts. Simmer long enough to heat the peas or sprouts (about 2 minutes). Arrange attractively on a heated platter.

Yield: 4 servings.

Each serving, including the vegetables, provides: 403.6 cal, 26.9 g pro, 3.58 g sat fat, 6.27 g unsat fat, 109 mg sodium, 50 mg chol.

Sautéed Trout

Serve with whole-wheat dinner rolls and a salad of grated carrots and zucchini sprinkled with balsamic vinegar—and you have a romantic dinner for two.

1 trout (about 1 pound)

$^1/_4$ cup low-calorie Italian dressing or your own, made with olive oil, vinegar, and herbs

1 slice whole-grain bread, made into crumbs

$^1/_4$ cup oat bran

1 teaspoon butter

1 teaspoon olive or canola oil

Rinse the fish under cold running water and pat dry with paper towels. Place the fish in a shallow bowl and add the dressing. Turn the fish to coat all sides. Leave it in the marinade for 15 minutes. Spoon the dressing over it several times. In a separate bowl, or on a double piece of wax paper, place the bread crumbs, mixed with the oat bran. Dredge the fish in this mixture, then refrigerate about 5 minutes. This will help the crumbs to "set."

In a heavy skillet, heat the oil and butter. Sauté fish until golden on one side; turn and continue to cook for a total time of 10 minutes per inch of thickness, measured at the fish's thickest part. If the fish is less than 1 inch at its thickest part, cook only until it flakes easily when tested with a fork.

Yield: 2 servings.

Each serving provides: 240 cal, 28 g pro, 4 g sat fat,
3.87 g unsat fat, 60 mg sodium, 50 mg chol.

Mackerel

When the mackerel make their first appearance of the season on the fish counter, you know it must be spring. Their high fat content enables them to take the winter off and just hibernate.

When fresh, mackerel have a lovely blue-green iridescence. Their flavor is distinctive and slightly gamey—which is why it tastes best when prepared with a slightly acidic sauce. Compared to the cost of other fish on the market, mackerel gives your wallet a break. And, of all fish, mackerel has the highest proportion of Omega-3 fatty acids, which have been shown to lessen the incidence of coronary heart disease.

Most mackerel hang out in northern waters and in the Mediterranean. The big daddy of the family, the kingfish— more accurately known as the king mackerel, weighing in at as heavy as 70 pounds—likes to winter down south, around both the eastern and western coasts of Florida.

Good "stand-ins" that can be substituted for mackerel in the following recipes are bluefish, butterfish, trout, and fresh herring.

Swedish Grilled Mackerel

This treat fills the air with an appetite-teasing aroma.

4 mackerel ($^3/_4$ to 1 pound each)

2 tablespoons olive or canola oil

1 tablespoon lemon juice

$^1/_2$ cup chopped onion

1 teaspoon Dijon mustard

2 tablespoons chopped dill

1 tablespoon chopped chives

1 teaspoon herbal seasoning

$^1/_2$ teaspoon freshly ground pepper

2 tablespoons butter, melted

Place the washed-and-dried fish in a shallow glass dish.

In a small bowl, combine the oil, lemon juice, onion, mustard, dill, chives, herbal seasoning, and pepper. Pour the marinade over the fish and allow fish to marinate for 1 hour, turning them once.

Place the fish on oiled grill. Brush both sides of the fish with the melted butter. Grill 3 inches above the white-hot coals for 4 minutes. Turn and grill the flip side for 6 minutes or until fish flakes easily when tested with a fork.

Yield: 4 servings.

Each serving provides: 256 cal, 21.9 g pro,
6 g sat fat, 12 g unsat fat, 101 mg sodium, 40 mg chol.

Baked Mackerel with Vegetables

Here is a wholesome, economical meal to serve a merry party of eight. The vinegar cuts the high-fat flavor of the fish. The vegetables provide fiber, vitamins, and minerals.

two 2-pound mackerel

1 large onion, chopped

1 large carrot, sliced

$^1/_2$ green pepper, chopped

$^3/_4$ cup wine vinegar

1 tablespoon chopped parsley

$^1/_4$ teaspoon dried thyme

1 bay leaf

Wash the fish and dry with paper towels. Place them in a shallow glass baking dish, lined with parchment paper or sprayed with non-stick cooking spray.

In a saucepan, combine the onion, carrot, pepper, and vinegar. Mix thoroughly; then add the parsley, thyme, and bay leaf. Add just enough fish stock or water to cover. Simmer for 10 minutes. Remove the bay leaf.

Pour the sauce over the fish. Bake in a 400-degree oven for about 15 to 20 minutes, or until fish flakes easily when tested with a fork. Serve fish and sauce in the dish you baked them in.

Yield: 8 servings.

Each serving provides: 162 cal, 11.4 g pro, 2 g sat fat, 5.3 g unsat fat, 96 mg sodium, 40 mg chol.

Mackerel Salad

Canned mackerel makes it possible to enjoy the flavor and health values of this fish when it isn't available in the marketplace. It also provides a meal that doesn't put a dent in your wallet. Mackerel is canned with water, and salt is added. If you are on a low-salt diet, rinse the fish with cold water before combining it with the other ingredients.

2 tablespoons white wine, tarragon, or balsamic vinegar

1 teaspoon Dijon mustard

1 clove garlic, minced

1 tablespoon olive or canola oil

2 tablespoons minced parsley

2 tablespoons snipped chives or scallions

$1/4$ cup chopped red onion

1 teaspoon minced fresh tarragon or $1/4$ teaspoon dried

one 15-ounce can of mackerel, drained and flaked *(Crush the bones. Do not discard them. They are an excellent source of calcium.)*

1 cup thinly sliced cucumbers or radishes, or a combination

1 head romaine or Boston lettuce

1 cup watercress leaves or parsley

In a medium-size glass bowl, combine the vinegar, mustard, garlic, and oil. Whisk to blend ingredients. Stir in the parsley, chives or scallions, and onions. Add the mackerel and toss gently. Cover and refrigerate for about an hour.

When ready to serve, add the radishes or cucumbers to the mackerel. Line a large salad plate with romaine or Boston lettuce, torn in bite-size pieces and combined with the watercress leaves or parsley. Place the mackerel salad on the greens. Garnish with parsley sprigs.

Yield: 4 servings.

Each serving provides: 150 cal, 11.4 g pro, 3 g sat fat,
7.3 g unsat fat, 90 mg sodium, 40 mg chol.

Bluefish

A member of the sea bass family, bluefish is a beautiful, feisty fish that weighs in at 2 to 25 pounds. It is named for the bluish-gray tint of its full-flavored, slightly sweet flesh that takes well to acidic sauces. It is high in protein, moderately fatty, and a good source of the wonder-working Omega-3 fatty acids.

Mackerel can be substituted for bluefish in the following recipes.

Baked Bluefish Fillets with Peppers and Tomatoes

The tomatoes and vinegar provide just enough acidity to cut through the fat in the bluefish.

2 pounds bluefish fillets

1 teaspoon olive or canola oil

$^1/_2$ cup chopped green pepper

one 16-ounce can stewed tomatoes

1 teaspoon red wine vinegar

$^1/_4$ teaspoon coarsely ground coriander seeds

1 teaspoon Dijon mustard

$^1/_4$ teaspoon freshly ground pepper

Wash the fillets and dry with absorbent paper. Place them in a shallow glass baking dish.

In a skillet, heat the oil and sauté the peppers briefly. Add the tomatoes, vinegar, coriander, mustard, and pepper. Stir and spoon over the bluefish. Bake in a 400-degree oven for 12 to 15 minutes, or until flesh flakes easily when touched with a fork.

Yield: 6 servings.

*Each serving provides: 247 cal, 21.1 g pro, 2.4 g sat fat,
6.2 g unsat fat, 172 mg sodium, 59 mg chol.*

Curried Bluefish with Zucchini and Yogurt

Here's a dieter's delight: a lovely high-fiber, low-calorie meal in a dish!

1 teaspoon olive or canola oil

1 large onion, chopped

2 cups thinly sliced zucchini

1 tablespoon curry powder

$1/2$ teaspoon freshly ground pepper

2 pounds bluefish fillets

1 cup plain yogurt

$1/4$ cup minced green onion

2 tablespoons sesame seeds

$1/2$ teaspoon paprika

Spray a large, non-stick skillet with non-stick cooking spray. Heat 1 teaspoon oil. Add onion, zucchini, curry powder, and pepper. Stir and cook over moderate heat for about 10 minutes. Set aside.

Spray with non-stick cooking spray a shallow glass baking dish large enough to accommodate the fish in a single layer.

Drain the zucchini mixture, reserving the drained-off liquid. Add this liquid to the yogurt along with the minced onion. Combine the zucchini mixture with the yogurt mixture and spread it evenly over the fish. Sprinkle with the sesame seeds. Dust with the paprika. Bake in a 400-degree oven for about 15 minutes, or until fish flakes easily when tested with a fork.

Yield: 6 servings.

Each serving provides: 165 cal, 22.6 g pro, 2.9 g sat fat, 3.5 g unsat fat, 70.5 mg sodium, 59 mg chol.

Tuna

We're all familiar with the flavor and convenience of canned tuna. Over a billion cans are sold annually in the United States. The largest member of the mackerel family, some tuna weigh in at 1,000 pounds—most of which goes directly to the cannery.

Fortunately, some of that tuna will bypass the cannery and go directly to the fish markets, where it is available to you. And believe me, if you've never tried fresh tuna, you're missing out on a simply sensational food experience, as well as a most delicious source of protein, vitamins, and minerals. Here are several different ways to prepare it.

Tuna Steaks with Ginger and Garlic

I like to serve with these as side dishes a high-fiber combo of brown and wild rice and steamed cauliflower.

2 tablespoons minced ginger root

4 large cloves of garlic, minced

2 tablespoons dry white wine

2 tablespoons sodium-reduced soy sauce

1 teaspoon herbal seasoning

$1/2$ teaspoon freshly ground pepper

$1/4$ teaspoon honey

4 tuna steaks, about $1/2$ inch thick

In a Pyrex baking dish large enough to accommodate the steaks in one layer, combine the ginger root, garlic, wine, soy sauce, herbal seasoning, pepper, and honey. Add the tuna steaks. Let them marinate for 15 minutes, turning them over several times.

Place the steaks in a preheated broiler or grill and grill for about 2 minutes on each side, or until just cooked through. Do not overcook. Serve immediately on heated plates.

Yield: 4 servings.

Each serving, without the side dishes, provides: 180 cal, 30.24 g pro, .12 g sat fat, .12 g unsat fat, 85 mg sodium, 63 mg chol.

Tuna Burgers

Serve these at your next patio picnic. Your weight-watching, health-minded guests will bless you. You can make the ginger juice by grating a 2-inch piece of fresh ginger.

$1^1/_2$ pounds fresh tuna, finely chopped

1 teaspoon ginger juice

3 tablespoons finely minced red onion

1 teaspoon reduced-sodium soy sauce

1 tablespoon chopped cilantro or parsley

1 tablespoon olive or canola oil

$^1/_2$ teaspoon Tabasco®

1 teaspoon herbal seasoning

$^1/_4$ teaspoon freshly ground pepper

1 teaspoon oil for brushing burgers and grill

In a bowl, combine the tuna with the ginger juice, minced onion, soy sauce, cilantro or parsley, oil, Tabasco®, herbal seasoning, and pepper. Shape the mixture into 4 patties and place in freezer for about 10 minutes.

Brush the burgers on both sides with oil and oil the grill. Grill over high heat for 2 minutes. Turn carefully and grill the other side for 1 minute, or until the burgers are seared on the

outside. They will be almost raw on the inside. Serve on toasted burger rolls with lettuce, tomatoes, and lemon wedges.

Yield: 4 servings.

Each serving, without the roll, provides: 205 cal, 35 g pro,
1.12 g sat fat, 6.12 g unsat fat, 50 mg sodium, 63 mg chol.

Barbecued Tuna with Balsamic Vinegar

This is a most savory dish. Serve it with pasta and a salad.

2 tuna steaks, about 5 ounces each,
or one large steak cut in half

1 tablespoon olive oil

2 tablespoons balsamic vinegar

$1/4$ cup fresh cilantro or parsley, finely chopped

1 clove garlic, minced

1 teaspoon herbal seasoning

$1/4$ teaspoon freshly ground pepper, or to taste

oil for the grill

Rinse the tuna, then poke several holes on both sides to aid in absorbing the marinade.

Make a marinade by combining the oil, vinegar, cilantro or parsley, garlic, herbal seasoning, and pepper. Place the tuna in a small bowl and pour the marinade over it. Let it marinate for 20 minutes.

Brush the grill with oil to prevent sticking. When the grill is hot, drain the tuna and place it on the grates for 1 minute. Lift the tuna and make a quarter-turn on the same side. This will help prevent the fish from sticking, and will make an attractive cross-hatch pattern on the steaks. Grill 3 more minutes, then turn over and repeat the process.

Yield: 2 servings.

*Each serving provides: 185 cal, 35 g pro, 1.12 g sat fat,
6.12 g unsat fat, 40 mg sodium, 63 mg chol.*

Swordfish

Even if you are an avid fisherman, I doubt that you'll ever find a swordfish nibbling at your bait. They can weigh up to 600 pounds. But you may find luscious swordfish steaks in your fish market. Its flesh is firm, dense, and flavorful (reminiscent of veal).

Swordfish takes well to marinades and lusty seasoning. It is wonderful grilled, broiled, baked, or stir-fried.

The following recipes will help you expand your swordfish horizons.

Parks' Swordfish
with Lemon–Rosemary Marinade

We enjoyed this succulent dish at Parks' Seafood, in Allentown, Pennsylvania, my favorite restaurant. Fred Parks, owner and creative genius, graciously shared this recipe with me.

6 swordfish steaks (approximately 2$^1/_2$ to 3 pounds total)

2 tablespoons olive oil

1 tablespoon shallots

1$^1/_2$ tablespoons lemon juice

$^1/_2$ teaspoon ground white pepper

$^1/_2$ teaspoon onion salt

$^1/_4$ teaspoon dried tarragon

$^1/_4$ teaspoon dried rosemary

In a skillet, sauté the shallots lightly in the heated oil. Add the wine, lemon juice, and seasonings. Heat just till warm in order to extract the flavors. Cool to room temperature; then marinate the steaks in it for approximately 20 minutes.

Using two wide spatulas, transfer the swordfish to an oiled baking dish large enough to hold them without overlapping.

Bake at 400 degrees for 10 minutes per inch of thickness, measured at the thickest part, or until fish flakes easily when

touched with a fork. Baste with the marinade several times during the baking process.

Yield: 6 servings.

*Each serving provides: 185 cal, 19.4 g pro,
3 g sat fat, 7.4 g unsat fat, 90 mg sodium, 50 mg chol.*

Grilled Swordfish Citron

And now for a medley of delectable flavors...

$^1/_2$ cup orange juice

$^1/_4$ cup lemon juice

1 tablespoon olive oil

1 teaspoon herbal seasoning

$1^1/_2$-inch piece fresh ginger, peeled and minced

1 large clove garlic, minced

$^1/_8$ teaspoon cayenne pepper

6 swordfish steaks (5 to 6 ounces each)

To grill, prepare a hot charcoal fire.

Meanwhile, combine the juices, oil, herbal seasoning, ginger, garlic, and cayenne in a shallow glass casserole. Mix till well blended. Marinate the swordfish in this at room temperature for 20 minutes, turning several times.

Place the fish on an oiled cooking grid set about 4 inches above the hot ashes. Grill for 6 minutes, then turn, brush with marinade, and grill for about 4 minutes longer, or until fish flakes easily when touched with a fork.

Yield: 6 servings.

Each serving provides: 203 cal, 21 g pro, 2 g sat fat, 5 g unsat fat, 50 mg sodium, 50 mg chol.

Stir-Fried Swordfish
with Water Chestnuts

This recipe also works well with other firm-flesh fish such as salmon, tile, or tuna. Serve with hot brown rice studded with chopped, toasted almonds.

1 cup vegetable or fish broth
1 tablespoon reduced-sodium soy sauce
1 tablespoon cornstarch
$1/4$ teaspoon hot pepper sauce
2 tablespoons olive or canola oil
2 teaspoons finely chopped fresh ginger root
1 large clove of garlic, minced
one 8-ounce can of water chestnuts, drained and sliced
2 cups broccoli florets
1 pound fresh swordfish, cut into 1-inch chunks

In a small bowl, combine the broth, soy sauce, cornstarch, and hot pepper sauce. Set aside.

In a non-stick skillet or wok, heat the oil; add the ginger and the garlic. Cook and stir briefly (about 30 seconds). Add the drained and sliced water chestnuts and the broccoli; cook, stirring, for about 2 minutes. Add the swordfish chunks; continue cooking and stirring until fish is opaque.

Stir the sauce into the skillet or wok. Reduce heat to medium; cook covered for 2 minutes longer, until fish is just fork tender and broccoli is bright green, crisp, and tender.

Yield: 4 servings

*Each serving provides: 260 cal, 26 g pro, 4 g sat fat,
8 g unsat fat, 250 mg sodium, 50 mg chol.*

CHAPTER 6
MISCELLANEOUS FISH

Gefilte Fish

Maybe you've never tasted gefilte fish, but you are most certainly acquainted with Tevye and his devotion to "tradition" as depicted in the popular musical *Fiddler on the Roof.* While Tevye was singing, Golda was chopping. With a big wooden bowl in her lap and a metal cleaver in her hand, she was chop-chop-chopping the carp, pike, and buffalo: She was making gefilte fish for the Sabbath meal.

Tradition lives. In Jewish homes all over the world, gefilte fish is a traditional Sabbath and holiday specialty. But you don't have to be Jewish to relish a piece of gefilte fish smothered in sinus-clearing horseradish.

Of course, some things change. You can now buy it in jars or cans, some with salt, some with sugar, some jelled, some with all-white fish, some with a mixture of fish. But there's nothing like the kind that Momma made, the kind you make yourself. "Hard on the chopping arm, but good for the soul," my mom used to say.

When selecting the fish, consider fish with three different qualities: fat, dry, and flaky. Traditional choices are carp, pike, white, and, of course, a little buffalo. When you ask for buffalo, the fishmonger might direct you to the meat department. Actually, what Momma called buffalo is a freshwater bass with a little mouth. I guess it has the visage of a buffalo. (It is not generally available.)

Momma's Gefilte Fish

Various kinds of fish can be used. Polish-style gefilte fish calls for haddock, cod, or whiting. The haddock is desirable because it contributes to a firmer texture. Adding the onion skins gives the broth a lovely color. My Mom used carp, pike, whiting, and, when she could find it, buffalo (she called it buffel).

3 pounds fish (carp, pike, or whiting)

2 onions, grated (reserve 2 pieces of onion skin)

2 carrots, grated

2 eggs

2 teaspoons herbal seasoning

$1/_2$ teaspoon white pepper

$1/_2$ cup water

3 tablespoons ground almonds or whole-wheat bread crumbs

2 onions, sliced

2 carrots, sliced

water

Fillet the fish or have it filleted at the fish market. Retain the skin, bones, and heads. Using a grinder or food processor, puree the fish fillets. Remove this to a wooden chopping bowl. Using a single-blade chopper with a handle, continue chopping the mixture as you add the onions, carrots, eggs, 1 teaspoon herbal

(cont.)

seasoning, $^1/_4$ teaspoon pepper, water, and ground almonds or bread crumbs. The mixture should feel just slightly sticky.

In a large heavy pot or poacher, place the bones, heads, and skin in the bottom. Add the sliced onions, sliced carrots, 2 cups water, 1 teaspoon herbal seasoning, the remaining $^1/_4$ teaspoon pepper, and the onion skins. Cover the pot, bring to a boil, then lower heat and simmer for about 20 minutes.

Meanwhile, with moistened hands, shape the fish into ovals about 3 inches long and $1^1/_4$ inches in diameter and place them on wax paper. Bring the broth to a smiling roll and lower the fish into the broth. Make sure the boiling liquid almost covers the fish. If necessary, add another $^1/_2$ cup water. Lower the heat and simmer on a very low flame for 2 hours. Let cool in the broth.

Using a slotted spoon, remove the cooled fish to a serving dish. Remove the carrots and garnish each piece of fish with a slice of carrot.

Cook down the stock to concentrate it, adjust the seasonings, then spoon a little over the gefilte fish. Leave to "set," and serve cold with horseradish.

Yield: about 12 pieces.

*Each piece provides: 150 cal, 14.5 g pro, .3 g sat fat,
.9 g unsat fat, 68 mg sodium, 10 mg chol.*

Tuna Gefilte Fish

For those occasions when time is pressing, or the budget is tight, this Tuna Gefilte Fish is ideal.

1 can (7¹/₂ ounces) white-meat tuna

2 eggs

1 onion (reserve the skin)

2 tablespoons wheat germ

herbal seasoning and white pepper

4 cups water

2 medium-size onions, sliced

2 carrots, sliced

¹/₈ teaspoon white pepper

1 teaspoon herbal seasoning

(cont.)

In food processor, puree the tuna, eggs, grated onion, and wheat germ. Season to taste with herbal seasoning and pepper. Form into ovals or balls.

In a large pot, combine the water, sliced onions, sliced carrots, pepper, and herbal seasoning. Bring to a boil, then reduce heat and simmer for 20 minutes. Place the tuna balls into the stock. Cover and simmer over low heat until the vegetables are soft—about 30 minutes. Allow the fish to cool in the stock.

With slotted spoon, remove the fish to a platter. Place a slice of carrot on each. Concentrate the stock, then pour some over the fish. Serve with horseradish.

Yield: 8 appetizer servings.

Each serving provides: 90 cal, 9 g pro, 1.2 g sat fat,
1.5 g unsat fat, 30 mg sodium, 30 mg chol.

Seafood Linguine

If you avoid shellfish for religious reasons or because you question its safety, there are some new products on the market that mimic that taste and texture but are actually made from pollack, a fin fish. Sometimes these are called "Sea Legs." Another of the brands available is called "It's Not Crab!—It's Kosher Fish." It is pre-cooked and can be used in any recipe that calls for canned tuna; or you can use canned tuna for this linguine.

1 teaspoon olive or canola oil

1 teaspoon butter

2 medium-size tomatoes, cubed

2 green onions, sliced

4 cloves garlic, minced

$1/2$ cup chopped parsley

12 ounces of "It's Not Crab!" or "Sea Legs"

2 tablespoons lemon juice

2 tablespoons fresh thyme, chopped, or 1 teaspoon dried

$1/2$ teaspoon freshly grated pepper

1 package linguine, cooked and drained

(cont.)

In a large non-stick skillet, heat the oil and butter. Gently
sauté the tomatoes, onions, and garlic for about 2 minutes. Do
not let the garlic brown. Stir in the parsley, fish, lemon juice,
thyme, and pepper. Simmer for another 2 minutes. Stir in the
cooked linguine. Can be enjoyed hot or cold.

Yield: 8 servings.

Each serving provides: 240 cal, 22 g pro, 2.5 g sat fat,
5 g unsat fat, 17 mg sodium, 41 mg chol.

Smoked Fish

My friend Arnie Lichtman is a master of the art of smoking fish and, I must admit, Arnie's fish has a marvelous flavor.

How do you prepare smoked fish? If you have an outdoor grill—no problem.

First, soak two handfuls of hickory chips in water. Then, start a charcoal fire. When the coals are glowing and covered with gray ash, take a few hickory chips, shake off excess water, and add them to the hot coals.

Brush the grill and the fish with oil or spritz them with non-stick cooking spray. Place the fish, skin side down, on the greased grill over the coals. Cover and smoke for 20 minutes to an hour, depending on the thickness of the fish, or until fish flakes easily and has a pleasant smoked aroma and flavor.

During the smoking process, add hickory chips to the fire to keep up a steady supply of smoke.

Now invite the neighbors—or your extended family—to share the feast. All cares and worries go up in smoke!

Smoked Salmon

Even if you don't have access to an outdoor grill, you can enjoy smoked fish. I used salmon for this dish, but you can use bluefish, mullet, perch, pompano, pike, tuna, or just about any kind available. Use a heavy cast-iron Dutch oven. Line the bottom with several layers of aluminum foil crimped up to about 1 inch off the bottom. Place the smoking ingredients on top of this platform. The ingredients you select depend on the flavors you wish to capture. Here's what I used.

2 teabags (any strong-flavored tea)

3 sprigs thyme

3 sprigs oregano

zest of one orange

$2^{1}/_{4}$-inch slices ginger root

1 cinnamon stick

2 tablespoons brown rice

Put the lid on the Dutch oven and raise the heat to "high." When it begins to smoke, about 3 minutes, set a steamer basket that's been spritzed with non-fat cooking spray over the smoke and put the rinsed and dried fish in it. Put the lid on and allow it to smoke for about 10 minutes.

Remove the Dutch Oven from the burner and let it sit for about 5 minutes. Serve with brown rice flavored with a bit of saffron or turmeric for a lovely golden color.

Marinade for Smoked Fish

This very tasty marinade can be used for any fish, even one prepared by methods other than smoking.

$1/_4$ cup balsamic or red-wine vinegar

$1/_2$ teaspoon cinnamon

$1/_4$ teaspoon powdered cloves

$1/_2$ teaspoon grated ginger root or $1/_4$ teaspoon powdered

2 tablespoons low-sodium soy sauce

freshly grated nutmeg

$1/_4$ teaspoon freshly ground pepper

Combine all ingredients and pour over the fish. Let the fish marinate for about 30 minutes. Then follow the procedure for smoking fish.

CHAPTER 7
ACCOMPANIMENTS:
SIDES AND SAUCES

The side dishes and sauces you serve with your fish should also be "smart." That means, of course, that they must contribute nutrients as well as flavor, and not throw a monkey wrench into your efforts at weight control.

Here are some of my favorites.

Horseradish Sauce

This is a satisfying, lusty complement to your broiled, baked, or sautéed fish. It's also a lovely salad dressing.

1 cup yogurt
2 tablespoons prepared horseradish (red or white)
2 tablespoons minced green onion or chives

Combine all ingredients in a pretty glass bowl. Refrigerate for at last 30 minutes to give flavors a chance to meld.

Yield: a little more than 1 cup.

Each tablespoon provides: 8.4 cal,
.5 g pro, .1 g sat fat, .1 g unsat fat, 9 mg sodium, 0 mg chol.

Creole Sauce

This sauce doubles as a zingy salad dressing.

1 onion, chopped
1 large tomato, chopped
1 hot pepper, chopped
2 garlic cloves, finely minced
1 teaspoon herbal seasoning
$1/_4$ teaspoon freshly ground pepper
juice of 1 lime
2 teaspoons olive or canola oil
fresh parsley

In a bowl, combine all the ingredients. Let the mixture stand at room temperature for about one hour. Serve raw, with lightly sautéed or poached fish.

Yield: about $1^1/_2$ cups or about 8 servings.

Each serving provides: 19 cal, .4 g pro, .2 g sat fat, .5 g unsat fat, 1 mg sodium, 0 mg chol.

Sweet Potato in Orange Baskets

A beautiful side dish, this is rich in flavor and nutrients, especially beta-carotene and vitamin C—two very important anti-oxidants.

8 oranges

1 pound sweet potatoes, boiled, baked, or microwaved, peeled and mashed

2 large eggs

1 cup milk

grated zest and juice of 1 lemon

2 tablespoons molasses or honey

Cut the top quarter off each orange, then hollow oranges with a grapefruit scorer or a melon-baller.

In a bowl, blend the scooped-out orange segments with the sweet potatoes, eggs, milk, lemon, and molasses or honey.

Fill each orange shell with the sweet-potato mixture. Bake for 20 minutes.

Yield: 8 servings.

*Each serving provides: 97 cal, 4 g pro, 1 g sat fat,
.9 g unsat fat, 56 mg sodium, 60 mg chol.*

Barley–Mushroom Casserole

Here's a truly delectable gourmet casserole to serve with fish. Barley is believed to be the first grain utilized by man. Pearled barley lacks the bran and germ of the original grain, so it cannot qualify as a whole grain. But a North Dakota organic farmer has made available his hull–less (it grows that way) unpearled barley; that's the kind I used in the preparation of this dish.

1 teaspoon herbal seasoning

2 cups cooked barley

$^1/_2$ cup chopped onion

$^1/_4$ cup chopped green pepper

$^1/_2$ pound mushrooms, sliced

2 teaspoons olive or canola oil

$^1/_4$ teaspoon freshly ground pepper

$^1/_4$ teaspoon sage

Stir the herbal seasoning into the barley. Set aside.

In a skillet, heat the oil and lightly sauté the onions, pepper, and mushrooms, stirring occasionally. Stir in the pepper, sage, and cooked barley. Cook over low heat for 5 more minutes.

Place the barley mixture in a $1^1/_2$-quart casserole. Bake, uncovered, in a preheated 350-degree oven for 25 minutes. Serve hot as an accompaniment to fish.

Yield: 6 servings.

Each serving provides: 126 cal, 3.7 g pro, .5 g sat fat, .3 g unsat fat, 16 mg sodium, 0 mg chol.

Pistachio Pasta Salad with Oregano Dressing

Oregano means "joy of the mountain." This salad will bring joy to your taste buds.

6 ounces rotini or shell macaroni
boiling water
Oregano Dressing
2 cups torn fresh spinach
1 cup chopped tomato
1 cup blanched pea pods
$^1/_4$ cup chopped shelled pistachios
Parmesan cheese (optional)

Cook the rotini or macaroni in the boiling water according to package directions. Drain.

To make the dressing, simply combine all ingredients.

OREGANO DRESSING

$^{1}/_{4}$ cup olive oil
$^{1}/_{4}$ cup red-wine vinegar
$^{3}/_{4}$ teaspoon crushed dried oregano
$^{1}/_{8}$ teaspoon garlic powder

Marinate the hot rotini or macaroni in the Oregano Dressing. Cool to room temperature. Combine with spinach, tomato, pea pods, pistachios, and pepper. Sprinkle with Parmesan cheese, if you choose to use it.

Yield: 8 servings.

Each serving provides: 100 cal, 4 g pro, .4 g sat fat, .5 g unsat fat, 11.5 mg sodium, 0 mg chol.

Mandarin Rice Pilaf

This is a wonderful partner for a fish dinner. It takes a little longer to prepare, but the delight with which it is always received justifies the extra effort. Make it for a special occasion— or just make it, and dinner will be special.

1 tablespoon olive or canola oil

1 onion, finely chopped

2 cups raw brown rice

2 cups orange juice

2 cups boiling water

12 whole cloves

1 small piece stick cinnamon (about 2 inches)

$1/4$ teaspoon powdered ginger

3 tangerines or oranges, sectioned

$1/2$ cup raisins

$1/4$ cup sliced toasted almonds

In a large saucepan, heat oil and sauté onions until soft. Add rice and continue cooking for 5 minutes, stirring constantly. Add orange juice to boiling water; pour the liquid over the rice. Add cloves, cinnamon, and ginger.

Cover and simmer for 35 minutes, or until liquid is absorbed. Remove cloves (count them) and cinnamon stick. Stir in the orange or tangerine sections, reserving 6 for garnish. Stir in the raisins.

Place the rice in a serving dish and garnish with the reserved fruit and toasted almonds.

Yield: 8 servings.

Each serving provides: 255 cal, 5 g pro,
1.1 g sat fat, 1.3 g unsat fat, 11 mg sodium, 0 mg chol.

Potato Kugel

You can exercise your arm muscles and grate the vegetables by hand, or you can use the food processor and prepare the mixture in jig time.

2 cups raw potatoes, unpeeled, scrubbed,
grated, and drained

1 large onion, grated

1 large carrot, grated

2 eggs, beaten

$1/4$ cup wheat germ

$1/4$ cup oat bran

1 teaspoon herbal seasoning

1 teaspoon baking powder

$1/8$ teaspoon freshly grated pepper

3 tablespoons olive or canola oil

In a large bowl, mix together the potatoes, onion, carrot, eggs, wheat germ, oat bran, seasoning, baking powder, pepper, and 2 tablespoons of the oil.

Place the mixture in a well-greased and preheated 9 x 9-inch baking dish. Sprinkle the remaining oil over the top. Bake in a 375-degree oven for about 1 hour, or until top is crisp and brown.

Yield: 8 servings.

*Each serving provides: 106 cal, 4 g pro, .5 g sat fat,
9.2 g unsat fat, 19 mg sodium, 0 mg chol.*

Fried Green Tomatoes

This recipe is adapted from one by the Whistle Stop Café.

1 medium-size green tomato
herbal seasoning
freshly grated pepper, to taste
$^1/_2$ cup cornmeal
2 tablespoons canola or olive oil

Slice tomatoes about $^1/_4$ inch thick, season with herbal seasoning and pepper, and then coat both sides with cornmeal.

In a large skillet, heat the oil. Sauté the tomatoes until lightly browned on both sides.

Alternate method: Instead of frying, place the sliced and coated tomatoes in a greased baking dish. Sprinkle each slice with a few drops of oil, or spritz with cooking spray, and bake in a 350-degree oven for about 15 minutes.

Yield: 2 servings.

*Each serving provides: 175 cal, 3.5 g pro, 1 g sat fat,
6 g unsat fat, 2.17 mg sodium, 0 mg chol.*

Banana and Eggplant

Here we have an unusual combination—but a lovely marriage. Serve it once and every diner will beg for the recipe.

1 tablespoon olive or canola oil

1 medium-size eggplant peeled and cut into cubes

1 medium-size onion, sliced

3 bananas, sliced

1 can (15 ounces) low-sodium tomato sauce

3 tablespoons minced fresh marjoram or 2 teaspoons dry

1 teaspoon herbal seasoning

$1/4$ teaspoon freshly grated pepper

In a large skillet, heat the oil. Add the eggplant and onions and sauté until golden. Add bananas, tomato sauce, marjoram, herbal seasoning, and pepper. Simmer until eggplant is soft.

Yield: 6 servings.

Each serving provides: 82 cal, 1.7 g pro,
.3 g sat fat, 2.2 g unsat fat, 6 mg sodium, 0 mg chol.

Index